Earn
All
You
Can

Donald R. House

Praise for *Earn All You Can*

"Don House sees what I cannot and enriches me because of it. Agree or disagree, he offers thoughts from his economic lens that make me engage my own biases. For leaders with responsibility to interpret wealth, poverty, and life governed by moral standards this is reason enough to read this book."
—**Gil Rendle**, Senior Vice President, Texas Methodist Foundation

"When the General Conference of the Methodist Episcopal Church South restructured in 1866, one visionary action was to call for lay delegates in future conferences. Almost a century later a new section of *The Book of Discipline* was entitled 'The Ministry of all Christians.' Don House has enhanced the heritage of the House Family, which had included at least six Methodist preachers, through the ministry of leadership and teaching beyond the local church. In his book, *Earn All You Can*, readers are challenged to a deeper understanding of the growing gap between the rich and the poor."
—**John Wesley Hardt**, Bishop in Residence Emeritus, Perkins School of Theology, Southern Methodist University, Dallas, TX

"This treatise on wealth, its attainment and use, is the most interesting consolidation of scripture and theology I've ever encountered. Having been a part of many of the discussions mentioned, and struggling with current church and government, I gained a great deal of knowledge and became eager to do additional research into the topic.

This book and the treatment of its subject matter informs, reminds, and stimulates thought and dialogue. In my own case, it addressed many issues I've been struggling with for a long time. It reinforces my basic beliefs and has prompted me to question and study more and become engaged in helping others in different ways."
—**Michael E. Workman**, former Harvey Hubbell Endowed Professor in Industrial Distribution, Texas A&M University, College Station, TX

Earn All You Can

Getting Rich for Good

Donald R. House Sr.

Abingdon Press
Nashville

EARN ALL YOU CAN:
GETTING RICH FOR GOOD

This book is printed on acid-free paper.

Library of Congress Cataloging-in-Publication Data

Names: House, Donald R., Sr., author.
Title: Earn all you can : getting rich for good / Donald R. House, Sr.
Description: Nashville : Abingdon Press, 2016. | Includes bibliographical
    references.
Identifiers: LCCN 2015034236 | ISBN 9781501808401 (pbk.)
Subjects: LCSH: Wealth--Religious aspects--Christianity. |
    Economics--Religious aspects--Christianity--History.
Classification: LCC BR115.W4 H68 2016 | DDC 261.8/5--dc23 LC record available at
http://lccn.loc.gov/2015034236

16 17 18 19 20 21 22 23 24 25—10 9 8 7 6 5 4 3 2 1
MANUFACTURED IN THE UNITED STATES OF AMERICA

Contents

Acknowledgments
and Dedication

The development of this book extended over many years and benefits from conversations among many friends, including economists, church leaders, and family. I am grateful for the tolerance of the members of my Sunday school class by giving me the opportunity to test these materials over the course of several weeks in such a setting. The feedback I received from these class meetings has been invaluable. Although grateful for the time and tolerance, I am not at all surprised.

John Wesley, who established the original Methodist Societies in England, once wrote: "To be ignorant of many things and to be mistaken in some is the necessary condition of humanity" and "As to all opinions which do not strike at the root of Christianity, we think and let think."[1] It is in this environment that these types of explorations can take place.

The preparation time for the Sunday school lessons and the time required to transform them into a book was enjoyable for me and was kindly tolerated by my wife, Paula. She remains the perfect coach—providing encouragement but also presenting the opposing arguments for a more complete consideration of the issues. Without this

---

1. Quoted in *The Book of Discipline of The United Methodist Church 2012* (Nashville: The United Methodist Publishing House, 2012), 54, 55.

encouragement, I trust that the lessons would never have been developed and presented.

I dedicate this work to my parents, Mary and Morris House. Among many other things, my mother taught me the importance of discipline, grace, courage, and respect for others. We lost my dad last summer at age ninety-seven. He preached his last sermon at age ninety-six, and some believed that it was his best among his seventy-five years of preaching. His impact upon me and this work is incalculable.

Preface

The motivation for writing this book is based upon personal experiences—from conversations with friends with strong opinions. The first occurred in 1973 when I started teaching economics at a large university. A faculty member and his wife, during a reception for new faculty members, mentioned that they left their church (Presbyterian) because of its position on key social issues. The issue had nothing to do with sexual orientation, gun ownership, or immigration. It had to do with its position on the inequality of income and what should be done. The couple concluded that their denomination was antagonistic toward the wealthy, not because of sinful conduct, but because they were wealthy.

The second conversation occurred in about 1995 when a member of a nearby church railed against the rich. She asserted that in a country such as ours, no one should ever amass the wealth of Bill Gates. She viewed the success of Mr. Gates as a travesty. She held a dislike for him even though they had never met. The accumulation of substantial wealth was enough.

I am fully aware of wealthy families financially assisting congregations, and such gifts are celebrated. Yet are donors viewed as sinful people? It seems incongruous to welcome the wealthy into our churches, celebrate their support for the church, but then disparage their successes in accumulating their wealth. Do we encourage the accumulation of wealth when celebrating their gifts but also disparage their character because they have been successful?

I grew up in the middle of the middle class; my father was a Methodist minister in a small countyseat town in east Texas. I grew up in the 1950s and 1960s in a politically conservative setting. I attended a university with a dominant military history, and I served in its corps of cadets. I served in an airborne infantry company of the army national guard, completed a PhD in economics, and taught economics for seven years—then went on to an economics research consulting firm for the next thirty-five years.

During the past eighteen years, I became interested in the polity and social principles within The United Methodist Church. As an economist, I find that many of the governmental policy positions supported by well-intended leaders are not grounded upon an understanding of economics but instead are grounded upon weak reflections of scripture. For example, Christ's insistence upon caring for the "least of these"[1] motivates some leaders to support any government program seeking to support poor families even when such programs are destined to have little or no impact upon the poor and, in some instances, leave the poor worse off. The primary interest seemed to be upon the giver and not the receiver.

I am active in the church: studying the organizational structure and serving as a delegate to General Conference. Delegates number in the thousands, so this is not a unique experience. I have also served as a member of the budget committees at all levels of the denomination. Many have the same experience. I began teaching Sunday school in an adult class of university professors, professionals, retired ministers, and missionaries. Members include the politically conservative and liberal. Uniquely, the members enjoyed diverse opinions, discussions, and explorations of social issues, theology, and scripture. It served as a laboratory for inquiry where there were no boundaries. Most everything presented was challenged. Controversy was and remains welcomed.[2] This became a laboratory for thought and exploration.

My personal quest is an inquiry into the Christian teachings toward the rich and responsibilities toward the poor. Recently, there have been public references to the top "1 percent"—those families in the top 1 percent of the income distribution in the United States. Conversations between friends and family members occasionally start with these public

---

1. Matt 25:40.

2. A&M United Methodist Church, Lost & Found Sunday school class, College Station, Texas. The class benefits from several excellent teachers.

references and continue with the mention of hungry children attending school. Sometimes conversations turn to the numbers of homeless in our cities and the families struggling with the burdens of unemployment. It is said that if we took more from the very rich we could solve the problems of poverty. There are those among the poor, homeless, and unemployed who have responsibility for their present station in life. They lack the motivation to improve. The scriptures call to care for the "least of these" regardless of the reasons for their present conditions. Thus these conversations often end with the contrast between the rich and the poor and the implication that the rich could do more to support the poor without consideration of the circumstances.

Imagine such a conversation among members of the local chamber of commerce including a member of the largest Protestant congregation in the city. This one listens but remains quiet with really nothing to contribute. To this church member, these are not new conversations. This member feels unprepared and vulnerable. The member understands the call to care for the "least of these." Some of the other members of this large Protestant congregation belong to the "1 percent" and are expected to feel guilty about the present condition of the poor. Assigning responsibility to the families of hungry children is to be uncaring. The common presumption is that taking more from the rich would at most impose an inconvenience upon them rather than a sacrifice. In the interest of social justice, which is of paramount importance in the scriptures, taking more from the rich and giving it to the poor would be an expression of compassion to which there should be little objection—especially from a member of the large Protestant church. The church member remains quiet, vulnerable, and unprepared—as have I.

It took several years of reading and study to begin to understand how shallow these conversations tend to be. For me, it took considerable study of the scriptures. It included a review of the works of theologians and economists. It included the study of religious doctrine, including Judaism, Catholicism, and doctrine from one of our largest Protestant denominations. It took discussions and debates within Sunday school classes. It took discussions with clergy, serving small and very large congregations. It took more than a few years writing many drafts of these chapters. It took presentations of several Sunday school lessons to test some of the ideas contained in this book.

After several years of study, including communications with biblical scholars, assessments of church mission projects, statistical analysis of denominational decline, and evaluations of government programs assisting the poor and unemployed, the common understandings of key scriptures that formed our critical views of the rich, our deep compassion for the poor, and our unceasing quest to make long-term differences in the lives of those living in poverty began to be questioned. It seems that these common understandings of scripture are at odds with some of the theological foundations upon which the Christian church was built. It seems that our collective efforts to show compassion for the poor and to make positive differences in their lives dramatically changed in the 1900s with a departure from these theological foundations. The shallow understanding of the gap between the rich and the poor may not have served us well.

After dozens of controversial Sunday school lessons to very tolerant but inquisitive members, the competing ideas and views have been placed in better perspective. The scriptures no longer seem to support the modern emphasis on efforts to temporarily ease the burdens of poverty rather than the historical emphasis on lifting people out of poverty. The scriptures no longer support the critical view of the rich but support a sense of appreciation and even admiration for the rich. The scriptures no longer support a shift in focus from the gap between the rich and the poor to a focus upon the numbers living in poverty—the causes and effective solutions. An increasing gap between the rich and the poor is viewed as an advantage in implementing solutions rather than evidence of a failure to care for the poor.

My renewed understanding of scripture in the context of economics, early American history, Judaism, Catholicism, and the Protestant expressions of Christianity prior to the 1900s, seems to make sense to most—but not all. The disparagement of the rich now seems unfounded and unjust. A growing gap between the rich and the poor is no longer discouraging. However, the development and implementation of public and private programs designed to temporarily ease the burdens of poverty appear much less productive and even destructive. Scripture predicts such consequences. Early theologians predicted such consequences. Economic studies suggest that the Christian church has suffered as a result.

Not everyone will agree with the ideas presented in the following chapters. Instead, I hope to broaden our knowledge of religious doctrine, understand our American historical efforts to implement the teachings from scripture, and consider perhaps a different perspective in evaluating the ways in which we seek to minister to the poor.

While I was in graduate school, an economics professor said to me that once he began to understand economic theory, he became a better Christian. His statement was startling at the time. I pondered the statement for more than thirty years. Through this recent inquiry, I began to understand his statement. This book tracks my own exploration in the apparent incongruence between economics and Christianity. I found that the answers to my questions were largely found in scripture. The explanations found in early Jewish writings; papal letters of one hundred years ago; and key sermons of John Wesley, founder of the Methodist societies in England in the 1700s, supplied the answers. Unfortunately, I could not find these materials presented in one convenient text so that others could explore my assembly of materials. Thus, this book was written.

Introduction

Poor persons will never disappear from the earth.
—Deuternomy 15:11

P eople say that economists never agree, and on some issues, they are correct. As with all disciplines, there are competing schools of thought. For example, when examining the inequality of income and appropriate public policy, economists do not agree. I was trained as a neoclassical economist in the tradition known as the Chicago school of thought. The economist Milton Friedman, who taught at the University of Chicago, is a well-known example from this school. This perspective stresses the importance of individual freedom in society so that the individual's self-interest can be fully expressed.

Some leaders react to an emphasis on self-interest as the primary motivation for conduct. In their view this perspective paints the individual as self-indulgent, greedy, and lacking compassion. Business owners are assumed to seek advancement at the expense of others. There is too little room for Christ's teachings, because self-interested people do not behave toward others with love and compassion. Others are to be manipulated when it suits the individual's quest for money, position, influence, and power. Self-interested motivation, to some, is the antithesis of the Christian doctrine of service.

This common view of self-interest is a caricature and a misrepresentation of neoclassical economics. As will be presented in chapter 2, economists recognize the deep passion of those who care for the poor at great personal sacrifice and expense. Economics does not condemn this conduct, just as it does not condemn conduct that expresses no compassion for the poor. As a social science, economics makes no such value judgments. However, economics provides a useful perspective by which one can more objectively examine the challenges of poverty. Part of the benefit from reading these chapters is the deeper understanding of the gap between the rich and the poor when Christian doctrine and economics are combined in a conversation.

The following chapters begin with the usual contrasts between the rich and the poor. The conventional message is that the rich are too rich, and there are too many living in poverty. This message is frequently reported in newspapers, television and radio broadcasts, news items disseminated throughout the Internet, Sunday school literature, sermons, and presidential State of the Union messages. We are all aware of the message but, perhaps, not well versed in the facts.

The contrast between the rich and the poor is followed by a collection of perspectives from the economists. These economic perspectives can be compared with scripture, Jewish doctrine, and some key Catholic papal letters that informed Protestant doctrine. Some early economists and theologians taught very destructive economic principles—perhaps not as bad as the teaching of bloodletting in medicine, but close. Admittedly, there remains controversy among economists who debate income gaps and solutions, but there is a dominant school of thought that not only comfortably coexists with Christian doctrine but strongly supports Jesus's parables.

After exploring teachings from the economists, we examine early Judaism. The reader will learn that the destruction of the Temple in Jerusalem occurred shortly after Christ's death and resurrection, and resulted in the loss of valuable religious literature (the Mishnah and Talmud) during the early formation of Christianity. The parting of ways between Christianity and Judaism, in light of the fact that both Jesus and the Apostle Paul were well educated in Jewish Torah (law), may have been too severe. This part of the book builds upon this Jewish literature that might have had a greater influence in the development of Christian doctrine.

The lives of Jesus and the Apostle Paul are then reviewed in the context of some basic economic principles. For some, this material will be a stretch, because it paints a different portrait of the two from the perspective of a vow of poverty and the presumed humble conditions in which both lived. The discoveries from excavations of the city of Sapphoris, only an hour's walk from Nazareth, form a major part of an alternative perspective.

With these perspectives in mind, we turn to Catholic doctrine and the consistencies between it and Judaism's interpretations of Genesis and the nature of humanity. We find two important papal letters, one from Pope Leo XIII in 1891 and one from Pope John Paul II in 1991. Both are better understood in their historical contexts—one following the Industrial Revolution and the other following the collapse of the Soviet Union. These two letters reportedly had substantial impact upon the Catholics but were virtually unknown among Protestants.

The next stop is a review of Protestant doctrine as expressed in the sermons of John Wesley—who formed the practices and doctrines for the Methodist churches. Again, strong consistencies are apparent between the teachings in key sermons and hymns and Jewish doctrine. The consistencies are so strong that I made an inquiry into the presence of the "lost" Jewish religious literature in the college libraries attended by John Wesley, but the religious historians concluded that there was no such presence in these libraries, bookstores, private collections in England at the time. Nevertheless, the consistencies are there.

With the presentations from the economists and reviews of Jewish, Catholic, and Wesleyan doctrines, we examine key New Testament scriptures often cited in the disparagement of the rich, the disdain of a growing gap between the rich and the poor, and the focus upon missional efforts rather than missional results. The most often quoted parable is that of the camel and the eye of the needle—recorded in three of the four Gospels. Some will continue to hold their long-standing interpretations of this parable, but perhaps others will admit that there are alterative, persuasive interpretations based upon Jewish doctrine.

We are then prepared to review early American history and the principles employed in implementing programs seeking to help the poor. These programs were almost uniformly based upon letters from the Apostle Paul and designed more to lift people out of poverty and less to provide temporary, material comfort while people are impoverished. Some reported results of the programs are strikingly positive. Yet, the fuels of compassion turned to public responsibilities instead of private responsibilities in the interest of efficiencies and scale. Such is the history of American compassion.

The continuing development of our public war on poverty led to the publication of two important books: *Toxic Charity* and *When Helping Hurts*.[1] They are disturbing books in that they question the effectiveness of many public and religious programs seeking to help the poor. They criticize some of our favorite missions of local congregations and challenge Christians to return to the hard work of developing close relationships with the individuals we seek to serve—a common practice in early America. Especially, in the context of the preceding chapters, the messages contained in these two books seem to fit in our journey.

Hopefully, the reader will gain a religious perspective toward the rich that, at a minimum, continues to question the foundations that support many of our conventional/secular views. It is unfortunate that most religious people are hesitant to discuss these issues because discussions tend to be too political. Perhaps this book will redirect these discussions toward religious considerations as the dominant perspective.

---

1. Robert D. Lupton, *Toxic Charity: How Churches and Charities Hurt Those They Help, and How to Reverse It* (New York: HarperCollins, 2011); Steve Corbett and Brian Fikkert, *When Helping Hurts: How to Alleviate Poverty Without Hurting the Poor... and Yourself* (Chicago: Moody Publishers, 2012).

Chapter 1

The Rich, the Scriptures, and the Detractors

Show me the money!
—Jerry McGuire, 1996 movie

T wo common measures are used to identify the rich. The most frequently used is the measure of annual income. This is most often used because summaries of tax returns that contain reports of annual income are regularly published. The second measure is that of wealth. It represents the value of one's property, net of all debt obligations. One's wealth is often reported to banks when qualifying for loans but is usually kept confidential.

In general, those with considerable wealth have relatively high incomes because much of their wealth is invested in income-producing properties, such as stocks and bonds. There are exceptions, such as the rancher who makes little from cattle operations but owns valuable land. For the most part, the rich who are regularly condemned are those who have considerable wealth and enjoy the lifestyles that only the higher incomes can support.

In Mark's Gospel, Jesus contends that the poor will always be with us.[1] This scripture implies that the rich will also be with us. There will

---

1. Mark 14:7.

1

always be an inequality of income for a host of reasons. The common use of the term *rich* refers to those at the top—a relative term rather than some absolute standard. The rich in some parts of the world may have incomes that would not qualify them as rich in other parts of the world. The central point here is that there will always be those at the top, and their position at the top troubles many who have compassion for those in poverty.

Many have turned to scripture to disparage the rich. The specific scriptures cited are often the same and are usually pulled out of context. Consider the usual citations:

> Pay attention, you wealthy people! Weep and moan over the miseries coming upon you. Your riches have rotted. Moths have destroyed your clothes. Your gold and silver have rusted, and their rust will be evidence against you. It will eat your flesh like fire. Consider the treasure you have hoarded in the last days.[2]

> Where your treasure is, there your heart will be also.[3]

> The love of money is the root of all kinds of evil.[4]

Perhaps the most frequently cited scripture is from Mark:

> "It's easier for a camel to squeeze through the eye of a needle than for a rich person to enter God's kingdom."[5]

Taken out of context, this is a convincing set of New Testament texts. The Old Testament contains references too, but these taken from Proverbs have more to do with the quest for riches than the accumulation of riches:

> Don't wear yourself out trying to get rich;
>   be smart enough to stop.

---

2. Jas 5:1-3.
3. Matt 6:21.
4. 1 Tim 6:10a.
5. Mark 10:25.

When your eyes fly to wealth
　　it is gone; it grows wings
　　like an eagle and flies heavenward.[6]

Reliable people will have abundant blessings,
　　but those with get-rich-quick schemes won't go unpunished.[7]

When extreme wealth is pursued, one might contend that the quest for wealth is sinful, and success in its accumulation is sinful. Collectively, these scriptures can form a powerful message. However, there is more to the broader context from which these scriptures are drawn. We will return to the biblical texts on wealth in chapter 7.

How do the rich become rich? This is an important question because many form their attitudes toward the rich on the basis of the answer to this question. Under the aegis of the American dream, those who become rich do so through years of hard work, smart choices, and disciplined spending. Americans are apt to admire those who start with nothing and, through hard work, slowly climb up the ladder to join those at the top. Americans have less admiration of those who inherited considerable wealth.

There are many paths to the top. Economic studies tell us that hard work alone will not assure one of a high income. Markets govern the value of one's efforts, and markets are continually changing. Today, markets do not reward the work of unskilled labor very well. An unskilled laborer can work diligently for many hours a week and never break into the higher income brackets. There was a time when an owner/manager of a TV repair shop could do quite well, but markets have changed. Too few owners of TVs seek the services of a TV repair shop. The market no longer rewards these particular skills very well.

As a general rule, economic studies consistently prove that education and training improve one's income potential. There are exceptions but not many. Studies prove that income attainment is inhibited without certain life skills, such as diligence in getting to work on time, attending to duties while at work, attending to personal hygiene, getting along with coworkers, and maintaining standards of integrity and honesty.

---

6. Prov 23:4-5.
7. Prov 28:20.

Education is available publically and privately. Higher-quality education often requires qualification standards attained by inherited capabilities, diligent study, or both. Valuable training most often is attained by experience—on-the-job training. One begins at a position requiring few skills and, through diligence and hard work, one is promoted into positions requiring more skills and abilities that are developed on the job. Promotion might require changing employers and geographic locations. Those unwilling to change employers or locations are often limited in the attainment of more valuable skills.

Life skills are most often taught within the family. Some are learned through role models. Some communities have schools of etiquette that teach fundamentals of manners in more formal settings. Churches are places where honesty and integrity are taught and experienced. Scouts, boys clubs, girls clubs, little leagues, and a host of other community activities are often places where life skills are demonstrated and taught. The family, of course, is a proven venue for teaching most life skills.

Many economic studies provide useful information on the gap between the rich and the poor. The IRS publishes summaries of income tax returns that are used by a host of writers, commentators, and researchers. Many observers maintain views about the gap by pointing to injustice. Observers cite statistics that highlight the inequality of income and wealth:

> According to the United Nations Development Program (UNDP), 20 percent of the world's people in the highest-income countries account for 86 percent of total private consumption expenditures, whereas the poorest 20 percent account for only 1.3 percent (1998). For example:
>
> - The richest fifth consumes 45 percent of all meat and fish—the poorest fifth, 5 percent.
>
> - The richest fifth consumes 58 percent of total energy—the poorest fifth, less than 4 percent.
>
> - The richest fifth consumes 84 percent of all paper—the poorest fifth, 1.1 percent.[8]

---

8. United Nations Development Programme, "Overview," *Human Development Report 1998: Consumption for Human Development* (New York: Oxford University Press, 1998), quoted in *The Book of Resolutions of The United Methodist Church 2012,*

And

> The United Nations 2005 Human Development Report found that the 2.5 billion people living on less than $2.00 per day (40 percent of the world's population) account for 5 percent of global income. The richest 10 percent, almost all of whom live in the high-income countries, account for 54 percent of global income. The United Nations 2006 Human Development Report found "The world's 500 richest people have an income of more than $100 billion not taking into account asset wealth." That total exceeds the combined incomes of the poorest 416 million persons.[9]

Income inequality exists in the world on every continent, in every country, in every town, and in every family. It is a consequence of virtually every economic system established throughout history. The existence of income inequality encourages comparisons between the rich and the poor. Compassion is extended to the poor—a response well grounded upon Christian doctrine. For the rich, responses are not always gracious.

Perhaps we all have images of the rich that are not admirable. Some individuals flaunt their riches, apparently to make sure that the rest of us know that they can afford some things and we cannot. Some are obnoxious in their manners, showing benefits of privilege that they might not deserve. They may be few in number, but some of their actions are well entrenched in our memories. Some of us are moved to anger and frustration. At times, their conduct is disgusting.

What the conduct of these few cause most of us to miss is that there are very wealthy individuals who police these tendencies and blend into the assemblies of common folk. They are anonymous in their charities, reside in humble dwellings, and drive not-so-expensive automobiles. The friends that they keep are from all parts of the income distribution and find themselves comfortable in conversation with the poorest in the community. They are endearing but difficult to identify. Yet, their numbers are surprisingly large.

"Resolution 4051: The United Methodist Church, Justice, and World Hunger" (Nashville: The United Methodist Publishing House, 2012), 542.

9. *The Book of Resolutions of The United Methodist Church 2012*, "Resolution 4052: Economic Justice for a New Millennium" (Nashville: The United Methodist Publishing House, 2012), 547.

Consider the true story about a maid serving a fraternity house in a college town. She spent countless hours ironing shirts for the fraternity brothers over many years. Her expenses were minimal, but she saved close to $100,000 and invested her funds, capturing the benefits of large-scale portfolios. To some, she belonged to the wealthy class, receiving the advantages or loopholes commonly captured by those of means. She willed $80,000 in scholarships for fraternity brothers to come—students she will never know personally. Perhaps she is an exceptional, wealthy individual, but she represents many who blend into the community without visible distinction.[10]

There are the super wealthy, with assets in the billions. We do not often encounter these folk in the local grocery store or Wal-Mart. They reside in homes set aside in estates that even require permission to visit. Some have inherited these fortunes, but most have acquired these fortunes through hard work. Nevertheless, they exist, and live in ways distant from most of us. We do not know them personally, but we read about them from time to time.

It is common for these super-wealthy families to establish foundations to manage their fortunes. The directors of these foundations are usually family members who carry out the intent of those who donated the foundations' funds. They often support specific philanthropic causes, such as education, extreme poverty, medical research, hospitals, conservation, and hundreds of others. They come in all sizes, from the Bill and Melinda Gates Foundation (Microsoft) to the $2,000 directed fund in a community foundation that supports the local animal shelter. Most would agree that gifts from these foundations support charities that make the world a better place. There are millions of these foundations—large and small. Their works are widely appreciated.

The poor live in our communities and throughout the world. Especially beyond the borders of highly developed countries you find those in extreme poverty. Many die of malnutrition. They live on the margin, and it takes only a minor event to cause disease and death. We do not see these individuals unless we purposely travel to these impoverished places. But we hear about them.

---

10. The story was published in a local newspaper in the 1970s in Auburn, Alabama. The copy of the article has long since been lost, but these types of events remain in one's memory for decades.

The poor in our communities in the United States are largely different from those in extreme poverty in other parts of the world. Most are not at risk of malnutrition unless they voluntarily adopt an unhealthy lifestyle and diet. The opportunities are there to acquire a reasonably comfortable standard of living, but some do not take full advantage of these opportunities for a variety of reasons. Of course, some in our communities live among the poor through no fault of their own. Opportunities for improvement do not exist. To most of us, these persons truly represent "the least of these." When identified, they attract compassion and care from people of all income levels. Unfortunately, we are often separated by differences in lifestyles and custom so that their existence and attended needs are not easily recognized.

The contrast between the very wealthy and those in extreme poverty is stunning. Those in extreme poverty are living on $1.50 per day. Some of the very wealthy earn $3 million a day doing nothing but watching their existing portfolios' growth. Occasionally, an author or activist will make a calculation such as this: if the top 1 percent gave to the needy, it would rid the world of malnutrition, reduce the infant mortality rate dramatically, and ensure that millions have a safe, comfortable place to live. Others will claim that the wealthy control more than their share of the world's resources, leaving too little for those in poverty. Some believe that the accumulation of wealth is the primary cause of poverty. Some believe that the accumulation of wealth reflects a refusal to share sufficiently with others. Regardless, the consequence is a well established disdain for the wealthy.

There are those who have engaged in "shady" deals at the expense of others. There are stories of corrupt bankers who maneuver into positions where they can personally gain from foreclosure on properties soon to become valuable when the city approves the location of a new shopping mall or airport. There are stories of corrupt businesspeople who take advantage of partners unaware of grand schemes to get rich. Consider the movies in which such scenarios are dramatically played out by favored actors. There are reports of Wall Street brokers who manipulate stocks sometimes beyond the limits of the law. Take Bernie Madoff, who confiscated $50 billion from investors, as a recent champion of this strategy.

The disdain for the wealthy grows with every report, movie, novel, and play carrying the same type theme. To be sure, there are the wealthy who engage in disgusting acts who could improve the stations of life for millions who live in extreme poverty.

Chapter 2

Early Theologians and Economists

The occupation of the merchant and all that surrounds it is to be justly condemned, since it serves only the lust of gain and Mammon.
—St. Thomas Aquinas

The poor will always be with us, and compassion calls us to care for the poor. In doing so, we seek to understand the causes of poverty to help guide our efforts. There are those who seem to live in poverty for a lifetime. Among them are those who have disabilities or face barriers that make escape difficult or near impossible. There are those who remain in poverty because of a poor work ethic, a lack of education because of poor choices, a strong sense of entitlement, and a lack of respect for authority. There are those who visit poverty for a short time—entering poverty due to circumstance but escaping at the first opportunity. Then, there are those who will soon join the ranks of the poor. The causes of poverty are many, and the solutions to poverty are challenging.

Their journeys differ. There is always compassion for the poor, but the prescriptions for improvement and prevention differ depending upon the conditions of the individual and the perspectives of those rendering assistance. Escape from poverty among those with disabilities is unlikely. For those who are able, escape from poverty might require education, training, or the presence of opportunity. Compassion calls

9

upon different forms of assistance depending upon the specific needs of the poor. Yet recommended solutions are often uniform. Are we called to provide relief to the poor in the form of material goods? Are we called to enable the poor to escape their conditions and become financially independent of others? In providing relief to the poor, do we discourage them from becoming financially independent of others? Is this what we are called to do? What should compassion lead us to do? These are important questions, but there is a wide range of answers.

People do not agree upon the dominant causes of wealth and poverty. Unfortunately, the disagreements among caring people are sometimes aggravated by those quick to assign labels—liberal, conservative, progressive, feminist, racist, capitalist, Republican, Democrat, Christian, Baptist, Catholic, and a host of others. We live in a time in which honest conversation is infrequent. This makes our own exploration difficult but, nevertheles, important. It is useful to question our own perspectives and to fully understand the perspectives of others. Religious doctrine has shaped our perspectives, but religious doctrine differs between Jews and Christians and between Catholics and Protestants.

Our compassion calls us to consider both immediate relief from the primary difficulties of poverty (need for food, clothing, and shelter) and assistance in developing tools by which the poor can climb up the income scale out of poverty. The former solution is easy. The latter solution is more difficult. The former is often temporary. The latter is often permanent.

Escaping poverty requires success in finding employment that pays sufficient wages. Many in poverty face economic barriers—skills that do not match the needs of employers, attractions to crime, substance abuse, and the absence of firms seeking additional employees. Most are economic issues. It is difficult to assist the poor effectively without understanding basic economic principles. Unfortunately, economic principles have been and continue to be misunderstood.

What follows is a presentation of the history of economic thought in the caring for the poor and addressing the barriers faced by the poor. The early considerations of economic principles were those of theologians. Some understandings were later discarded, but they lasted for centuries. After the theologians, the early economists came with their own misunderstandings. A portion of these misunderstandings are championed by some of today's religious writers. The modern economists have, for the most part, corrected these misunderstandings but they still persist in many conversations and writings. Dependence upon these misunderstandings has made the implementation of effective solutions to poverty almost impossible.

The economic principles to be considered in this chapter are not difficult. Most readers will have more casually considered these principles before, but it is useful to recognize those who more formally developed them—particularly the theologians who shaped early Christian doctrine. We begin with the theologians in the twelfth and thirteenth centuries and then turn to the early economists in the nineteenth century. Our overview ends with recent works of economists in the past few years. -

Early Economic Thinking: Catholic Theologians

Johannes Gratian was a lawyer from Bologna, a city in northern Italy and home of the University of Bologna, the oldest university in Europe, founded in 1088. Gratian taught theology. His important work, *Decretum Gratian*, published in 1150, synthesized the varied religious writings of the time, seeking to provide uniform, consistent teachings of Catholic doctrine. He is said to have written the first complete organization of canon or moral laws for the Catholic Church. His work heavily influenced the continuing development of Catholic doctrine.

These moral laws included two features important to our inquiry: the charging of interest on loans and the determination of value or price. The charging of interest on loans was prohibited and loosely based upon scripture.[1] According to these laws, the intrinsic value of products is not to be determined in the marketplace. Instead, there is a higher process that determines value. According to Gratian: "Whoever buys a thing that he may gain simply by selling it unchanged... that man is like the buyers and sellers who were cast forth from God's temple."[2] The intrinsic

---

1. See Deut 23:19-20 and Exod 22:25.
2. Meir Tamari, *With All Your Possessions: Jewish Ethics and Economic Life*, Kupietzky ed. (Jerusalem: Maggid Books, 1998), 93.

11

value of a product is not fully explained, but it is clear that the merchant should not increase its price for public retail sale.

The prohibition from charging interest on loans is largely based upon the Old Testament. Medieval Jews did not adopt such a prohibition and were morally free to charge interest on loans. This difference between Judaism and Christianity is considered more fully in chapter 3.

After the publication of Gratian's work, in 1274 St. Thomas Aquinas published his *Summa Theologica*. St. Thomas Aquinas was a Catholic priest in Italy. The formal study of economics began centuries after his death, so St. Thomas could not benefit from the theoretical and empirical works found in much later economic studies. Nevertheless, he had a substantial impact upon some important religious perspectives about economic organization and activities that might have hindered economic development. His impact upon Catholic doctrine has been substantial. Pope Benedict XV referred to St. Thomas as "the master and patron of Catholic schools."[3] His influence upon Catholic doctrine was much more substantial than that of Gratian.

St. Thomas taught merchants or those engaged in trade that an importer of goods should not increase the price of those goods above the purchase price plus the costs of transportation. In essence, there should not be a monetary profit for the services of an importer or middleman. According to St. Thomas:

> It would seem that it is not lawful, in trading, to sell a thing for a higher price than we paid for it. For Chrysostom [*Hom.xxxviii in the Opus Imperfectum, falsely ascribed to St. John Chrysostom] says on Mat. 21:12: "He that buys a thing in order that he may sell it, entire and unchanged, at a profit, is the trader who is cast out of God's temple." Cassiodorus speaks in the same sense in his commentary on Ps. 70:15, "Because I have not known learning, or trading" according to another version [*Septuagint]: "What is trade," says he, "but buying at a cheap price with the purpose of retailing at a higher price?" and he adds: "Such were the tradesmen who Our Lord cast out of the temple." Now no man is cast out of the temple except for a sin. Therefore such like trading is sinful.[4]

---

3. He was born in 1854 and served as pope between 1919 and 1922.

4. Thomas Aquinas, *Summa Theologica*, 2 (New York: Benzigor Bross., 1947), 2023. His adoption of the labor theory of value, to be explained shortly, has been the subject of debate. Richard Henry Tawney's *Religion and the Rise of Capitalism*,

The concept of a free market did not widely exist in mediaeval Europe, which was dominated by feudalism, so for St. Thomas, the value of a product is determined by a process of passing along the cost of transportation and the price already assigned by the maker of the product. Perhaps because price gouging has always been a problem where demand for necessities exceeds supply, St. Thomas contended that the re-pricing of a product in the normal course of retailing is sinful. Observance of this moral law inhibited economic development among Christian communities since it inhibited international trade.[5] No distributor would import goods from other countries if the reseller could not increase its price to generate the margins necessary to remain in business.

Two economic principles were reflected in the works of these early Catholic theologians. According to their moral reasoning, retail markup pricing of products among merchants reflected greed and the quest for riches. Moreover, the charging of interest on loans was also a reflection of greed and it also was prohibited by moral law.

In our global economic culture a thousand years later, we know that retailers serve critical functions by bringing products to consumer markets. Without enough retailers, fewer products would be produced and much of our international trade would disappear. Retail pricing of products above what it cost to make the product is the essential method by which retailers recover their costs and earn the profits necessary to stay in business.

Interest charged on loans is necessary for banks and other financial institutions to pay interest on deposits, thereby encouraging saving. Loans provide the funding for building and home construction, utility systems such as water and electricity, and the building of new churches. From an economic perspective, interest payments for loans and deposits properly reward those willing to save and delay purchases and impose

---

published in 1926, reprinted in 1937, 36, concludes, "The true descendant of the doctrines of Aquinas is the labor theory of value."

5. Tamari, *With All Your Possessions*, 77–79. Tamari emphasizes the importance of the networking among Jewish communities across Europe, North Africa, and the Middle East. Without the moral restrictions faced by Christian merchants and financiers, Jews helped foster trade and the resulting economic development. Communities without these advantages were slow to develop beyond the feudal systems.

costs (interest payments) upon those not willing to spend the time to save sufficient funds for large projects. Without the payment of interest on loans, there would be no financial markets upon which growing economies heavily depend.

Early Economic Thinking: The Economists

In 1817, the economist David Ricardo published his famous work, *Principles of Political Economy and Taxation*. Among the economic principles contained in this text, Ricardo explained the labor theory of value. This theory argues that the value of any product is determined by the labor required to produce it. This has been an unfortunate concept, because it negates the role of market transactions in determining value and advances a notion of natural value determined by labor. It seems consistent with the Catholic moral law expressed by St. Thomas Aquinas that prohibits a merchant from increasing the price of a product in response to increases in demand.

Ricardo presented another economic principle that has persisted in some modern religious writings. This economic principle, which has not been accepted by economists over the past one hundred years, is known as the "wages fund theory." This is a concept of a fixed amount of surplus that is to be distributed to labor—a fixed fund from which all labor is paid. In the agricultural setting at harvest time, one can understand a context in which this has some merit, when the field hands get their fixed share of the proceeds as the crop goes to market. Yet, its use has been extended well beyond the harvest setting and is alive and well today.

Several years later, John Stuart Mill published his *Principles of Political Economy* in 1846. He, too, endorsed the notion of a wages fund. If one employee is paid more, others are necessarily paid less. The problem with the wages fund theory is that it pits one laborer against another in determining wages. As one employee is paid more, another is necessarily paid less. This does not account for the increasing productivity of labor, which largely sets the wage scales of labor.

Economists discarded the wages fund theory by the time of the Industrial Revolution. The Industrial Revolution reset people's understanding of the relationship between labor and capital. With the implementation of steam engines, labor in some industries became much more productive. With increases in productivity, skilled labor received increased wages relative to unskilled labor—much more than in earlier times. Economists began to understand that increased wages were paid in response to improved labor productivity. Some could be paid more without disturbing the wages of others because of increased productivity. This is a simple economic principle but one that is sometimes ignored—even today.

Modern Economic Principles: The Values of Products

The most basic principle in economics is the determination of value or price of a product or the value of one's labor. The familiar phrase "demand and supply" is fundamental today, but it has not always been so. The determination of value (or price) is recognized by economists for at least a century. The economist Alfred Marshall, in his *Principles of Economics*, first published in 1890, stands out above many. He was an English economist, teaching at Cambridge. His text was recognized throughout the world, and he is viewed as one of the founders of modern economics. It is important to note that his works followed that of two earlier economists, David Ricardo and John Stuart Mill, both noted earlier.

Alfred Marshall is credited with the first graphs of demand and supply, which is used in virtually every economic principles textbook and class since. Regarding the determination of price: "When demand and supply are in equilibrium, the amount of the commodity which is being produced in a unit of time may be called the *equilibrium-amount*, and the price at which it is being sold may be called the *equilibrium-price*."[6]

6. Alfred Marshall, *Principles of Economics*, 8th ed. (London: Macmillan, 1920), bk. 5, chap. 3, para. 19. The full text is available at http://www.econlib.org/library/Marshall/marP30.html#Bk.V,Ch.III.

This principle is almost universally accepted and displaces other theories of value that had previously existed, including the labor theory of value.

There are three key modern contributors to this important body of economic literature whom you should know: Friedrich Hayek, Milton Friedman, and Gary Becker—all winners of the Nobel Prize in economics. There are, of course, many others, but these are the ones that I would introduce to you if all were assembled at a single gathering.

Friedrich Hayek, an economist from Austria, wrote at a time when empirical investigation was limited (computers were not widely available), but he was a giant in explaining neoclassical economic theory— the free market theory tested by many economists to follow. Hayek has a unique perspective having seen firsthand the control of the German economy by the Third Reich, the control of Eastern Europe by Soviet Russia, the rebuilding of Western Europe after World War II, and the ascension of the United States to become the strongest economy the world has ever known. His most noted treatise is entitled *The Road to Serfdom*, published in 1944, but his other contributions to the economic literature are extensive.

Milton Friedman is perhaps the second-best-known economist in the world today—second only to John Maynard Keynes. He published extensively, wrote columns in newsmagazines for years; was the resident expert on a continuing TV special, *Free to Choose*; and was the chosen participant in many recorded presentations and discussions of his time. He served as an advisor to President Reagan as well as other world leaders. His work led several countries to adopt his recommendations of public policy, and their implementations have lifted millions out of extreme poverty. One of his most popular books is entitled *Capitalism and Freedom*, published in 1962. His chapter on the distribution of income is particularly useful.

Gary Becker greatly expanded our understanding of the benefits of education (or the accumulation of human capital), among other aspects of human behavior. As common among all serious economists, Becker emphasized the importance of economic incentives in explaining differing levels of educational attainment. There is considerable literature that demonstrates the impact of educational attainment on income and income inequality. Becker brought a deeper understanding of educational attainment and responses to changes in economic incentives. Now we can turn to more extensive discussion of their collective works.

Hayek understood the workings of free markets and the importance of economic opportunities placed before individuals. Economic markets develop as individuals find value in goods and services that others can produce. Many are willing to work in the production of goods and services that others are willing to purchase. For example, an entrepreneur finds that he or she can produce and sell fresh water to the residents of a village if he or she digs a well and builds the frame, pulley, and bucket with which customers can draw fresh water at their convenience. Residents would no longer have to walk back and forth to the river several times a day to obtain water. For a small fee they can conveniently draw water from the nearby well. The owner of the well earns an income from the new water business.

Hayek explains that through the ingenuity of entrepreneurs, a host of new products and services are developed that individuals find sufficiently valuable that they will find employment in order to earn the income necessary to purchase these new products and services. As markets for goods and services expand, the standards of living of people improve. Hayek observes the growth of economies as highly beneficial to humankind.

To Hayek, these improvements in standards of living are the product of free markets that require the establishment and compliance with certain rules of the game. Individuals must have sufficient confidence in the rule of law—the protection of property rights. The entrepreneur will build a water well only if the producer believes that the village elders will not take ownership away or prohibit charging residents for the well water. The residents willing to gather wild berries, fish, and hunt game to earn an income necessary to purchase well water must have confidence that they can freely sell berries, fish, and game in the local marketplace. And all individuals must have confidence that they can save and store money without the risk of theft or confiscation by the village elders.

Hayek heralds the entrepreneurs' imagination through which they invent new products, new services, and more efficient processes that benefit humankind. They do so for a host of reasons, but Hayek observes through history that the quest for profits is the major driver of invention and innovation. When the profit potential is eliminated (through the absence of a rule of law) or diminished (through burdensome taxation of profits), entrepreneurial activity is diminished, and society fails to benefit from the development of a host of new products and services. The entrepreneur's quest for profits might be called greed by some, but Hayek focuses upon society's benefits from the entrepreneur's willingness to risk much (sometimes everything) in hopes of earning a profit.

Hayek contends that the benefits society has gained from entrepreneurial activities are often not fully appreciated. Medical advances, less expensive and faster ground transportation, commercial flight, more effective and efficient means of communication, safe food and water, access to agricultural products from all over the world, inexpensive clothing, air-conditioning and heating, fire prevention, and much more. The innovations of more productive processes are rarely seen by the consumer, but the benefits are observed in lower consumer prices, such as the prices of automobiles, telephone service, electricity, gasoline, food, clothing, housing, books, televisions, computers, and much more.

Yet, it is the successful entrepreneur who financially benefits from these activities. It is the Bill Gateses of the world who accumulate substantial wealth. The gap between the income of the part-time, unskilled worker and the income of the most successful entrepreneur can grow larger and larger as the economy grows and new products and services are introduced that are highly valued by consumers. Hayek understood that the growing gap is a reflection that the economic engine is working better and better.[7]

Hayek's principles are meaningful in the context of free markets where property rights are enforced (i.e., the rights of ownership). In controlled economies, a few in power can regularly take from others and cause a growing gap between the rich and the poor. The unfortunate consequence is the broader contention that any growing gap reflects the use of power at the expense of others.

Among those benefiting from entrepreneurial activities are the poor. By definition, the poor have fewer means through which they can purchase goods and services in the marketplace, but what they can purchase with so little today is astounding compared to what was and

---

7. This conclusion does not apply to controlled economies. There are many historical examples in which dictators have prevented unencumbered mobility across the income classes. Peasants remain peasants.

is available in other places and other times. Our review of Hayek is introducing one of the challenges of religious doctrine: should the focus of religious doctrine be upon the accumulation of wealth through an emphasis of the notion of greed or should the focus be upon the true plight of the poor? The historical solutions to this challenge is not only interesting but important.

Hayek believed that the rule of law is alone not sufficient for sustaining growth in the economy. Hayek was an agnostic, being unable to personally believe in a divine creator but acknowledging that such could exist. Yet, Hayek believed that morals, over the centuries, have played a substantial role in the development and organization of societies that have propelled humankind to higher and higher levels of achievement and standards of living.[8] Certain sets of morals, transferred intact from generation to generation, have proven to be essential in support of freedom and the family. This support has proven imperative to humankind. Other sets of rules and behaviors, such as those adopted within communism or socialism, which are antifreedom, antifamily, and antireligion, have led to organizations of societies that have inhibited economic growth and improvements in standards of living for all.

> I sometimes think that it might be appropriate to call at least some of them [religious beliefs], at least as a gesture of appreciation, "symbolic truths." ... Even those among us, like myself, who are not prepared to accept the anthropomorphic conception of a personal divinity ought to admit that the premature loss of what we regard as nonfactual beliefs would have deprived mankind of a powerful support in the long development of the extended order that we now enjoy, and that even now the loss of these beliefs, whether true or false, creates great difficulties.[9]

For Hayek, religion plays a critical role in preserving that set of morals which guides humankind's conduct in a way that encourages economic growth and moves the poor in society to ever-improving

---

8. Without morals, trade and economic development would be inhibited due to consequences of cheating, lying, and theft. Economic development would be inhibited because even simple transactions could not be based upon trust but would require resource-absorbing, external enforcement of agreements.

9. F. A. Hayek, "Religion and the Guardians of Tradition" in *The Fatal Conceit: The Errors of Socialism* (Chicago: University of Chicago Press, 1988), 137.

standards of living. The preservation of individual freedom and the presence of a strong family unit are essential.

Hayek contends that support for the poor through income redistribution is destructive to economic growth. He cites several persuasive cases from history. Being originally from Austria, he personally experienced much of the impact of Soviet control over Eastern Europe and its contrast with the postwar development of Western Europe. For decades, Eastern Europe was largely devoid of entrepreneurial activities while Western Europe experienced the development of products competitive in world markets, such as German-manufactured automobiles, machinery, and heavy trucks. France emerged as a leader in fashions in apparel and many consumer products. These occurred after the virtual destruction of their economies and manufacturing capacities during World War II.

I recall attending a conference in Germany hosted by the German company Villeroy & Boch. The then president of the company was our host for an evening dinner when he spoke of their expansion into East Germany after the fall of the Berlin Wall on November 9, 1989. They invested in a new manufacturing facility in the former East Germany in order to benefit from the large pool of untapped German labor and to help improve unemployment in that part of the unified Germany. Much of Villeroy & Boch's production capacity was and is stationed in the former West Germany.

Not only did the president of Villeroy & Boch discover the absence of viable businesses within supporting industries, the condition of the German labor force in the former East Germany was insufficient. German laborers were not adept at the fundamentals of showing up for work on time or having the endurance of working forty hours a week over a number of consecutive weeks. These deficiencies were so substantial that employee training could not elevate labor productivity sufficiently over any reasonable period of time. The plant was closed.

Germany's experience with unification is a vivid demonstration of Hayek's warnings of government's limitations upon economic freedom. Such limitations restrict economic growth, which is the most productive vehicle by which individuals escape the conditions of poverty. This poses a challenge for some religious leaders. Hayek champions the successful entrepreneur whose inventions benefit humankind. Some religious leaders, upon observing financial success, are quick to suspect that in the quest for success the entrepreneur took advantage of his or her employees along the way.

The works of Milton Friedman consider ethical aspects of the inequality of income. Friedman proposed that society should seek the equality of treatment rather than equality of outcomes. Consider two individuals with equal abilities and conditions, but one values leisure time (jogging, vacationing, time with family) more than market goods (new cars, larger home, and membership in expensive clubs). The other values market goods more than leisure time. As for Friedman (and many others), there is no reason to disparage either of the two. Equality of treatment would mean that the individual who values market goods more must work late hours, forgo some allotted vacation time, and attend professional advancement seminars. These activities lead to higher salaries. The income-leisure packages received by the two individuals are actually the same—one enjoys more leisure time and the other enjoys more market goods.

Yet, there will be an inequality of income, measured strictly by salaries. One would have a difficult time ethically in taking income away from one and giving it to another in order to equalize incomes. This action makes treatment unequal.

Friedman goes further in explaining the importance of risk taking. In my line of work I have met many true entrepreneurs. I have observed the histories of entrepreneurs investing in graduate degrees that require the temporary sacrifice of post-graduate earnings during graduate school. I have observed the years of work in industries that provide the understanding and knowledge necessary for new ideas to develop. I have observed the loss of income security as they terminate employment in order to start their own firms. I have observed the investments from their retirement accounts, the refinancing of home mortgages, and living off savings while their new companies develop through the initial years of financial losses in the hope of earning profits before they deplete their personal financial reserves. I have observed some that have been successful and others that have failed. Both Hayek and Friedman describe the benefits society reaps in access to new products as a result of individuals choosing these risk-taking paths. We can easily observe the successful entrepreneurs, but the unsuccessful ones fade and are quickly forgotten. Both are consequences of entrepreneurial risk taking.

Friedman considers the importance of entrepreneurial investments in capital—plant, equipment, and operating funds. Successful investments lead to increases in employment, which is the primary pathway out of poverty. The entrepreneur always has to accumulate the financial resources to purchase or lease plant and equipment and to have the funds to weather the first few years of financial losses. Most entrepreneurs must borrow most of the funds necessary to get the new venture up and running. Friedman considers this puzzle with the illustration of games: a zero-sum game and a positive-sum game. A zero-sum game is like a flip of a coin in which two individuals gamble $100 each. There will be one winner and one loser. The winner will walk away with $200 and the loser will be $100 poorer. In sum, there is no gain. A total of $200 is bet, and $200 is won. The ownership of the funds is changed, but nothing is created.

A positive-sum game is different. Suppose the two individuals take their $200 and invest in seed, fertilizer, and labor to raise an acre of corn. At the end of the day, the corn is harvested and sold for $350. The game is a positive-sum game in that the $200 grew to become $350. The comparison is simple but extremely important.

The wages fund theory argues that as the rich get richer, the poor must get poorer. This is a zero-sum game result. However, if the rich get richer because of increases in productivity, the poor need not get poorer. This is the positive sum game result. Through increased productivity, the rich get richer but there is no requirement that the poor get poorer. Some may argue that a growing gap between the rich and the poor yet is still unfair, but this is a different argument.

In extending Friedman's emphasis on productivity, Robert J. Barro offers important empirical evidence of the typical path economies take in development.[10] The underdeveloped economy begins with heavy dependence upon agriculture. The gap between the rich and the poor is relatively small because there are few opportunities for anyone to accumulate significant wealth. As industry develops, entrepreneurs emerge and some are propelled to the higher income levels. The gap widens as many remain on the farms and some move to the cities for improved wages. A few become successful industrialists. In time, fewer and fewer

10. Robert J. Barro is a professor of economics at Harvard University. He has been ranked as the third most influential economist in the world. See *Research Papers in Economics*, August 2011.

remain on the farms, and more and more acquire skills that are handsomely rewarded in the growing industries. The gap then narrows as the economy grows with less dependence upon agriculture and more dependence upon industry.[11] This pattern is referred to as the Kuznets curve, attributed to Simon Kuznets—another Nobel Prize winner in economics.[12] Throughout the Industrial Revolution, there was a growing gap between the rich and the poor. It is not reasonable to conclude that this growing gap was detrimental to the poor or to society in general.

Gary Becker provided important clarity in the application of the standard assumption of self-interest as one's primary motivation. The concept of self-interest need not imply a narrow motivation to accumulate wealth for one's own consumption. Instead, self-interest includes any activity that promotes one's satisfaction or benefit. In his 1974 paper entitled "A Theory of Social Interactions," Becker argues that interactions with others is a recognized source of benefit to the individual.[13] He sets forth a mathematical model in which charitable giving is explained as a benefit to the giver. The amount one gives to others is positively affected by increases in one's income. The recipients of charity receive more as the incomes of givers improve. Additionally, the amount one gives to others is affected by the gap between the rich and the poor. The rich are encouraged to provide more charity to the poor when the gap widens. Given the incomes of the rich, if the poor become poorer, the rich respond with greater levels of charitable gifts. Becker thus introduces a reverse notion of greed. As the gap between the rich and the poor widens, the rich respond with greater gifts of relief to the poor. Charitable gifts to the poor are a consequence of self-interested motivation.

Becker greatly expanded our understanding of the attainment of education (or the accumulation of human capital), among other aspects of human behavior. As common among all serious economists, Becker emphasized the importance of economic incentives in explaining

11. Robert J. Barro, "Inequality and Growth in a Panel of Countries," *Journal of Economic Growth* 5, no. 1 (2000), 5–32.

12. Ibid., 10. According to Barro, "I find that the Kuznets curve shows up as a clear empirical regularity across countries and over time and that the relationship has not weakened over time."

13. Gary S. Becker, "A Theory of Social Interactions," *Journal of Political Economy* 82, no. 6 (1974), 1063–93.

personal choices. There is a considerable body of literature that demonstrates the impact of educational attainment on income and income inequality. Becker brought a deeper understanding of educational attainment and responses to changes in economic incentives.

In 2008 during meetings in Tokyo, Becker presented his coauthored paper with Kevin Murphy entitled *Globalization and Inequality*, later published as "The Upside of Income Inequality." In this important paper, he demonstrates the slowed growth in educational attainment in the United States—particularly between 1970 and 2000. Two major forces were at work: the weakening of the family structure and increased taxes on the wealthy. He demonstrates that increases in educational attainment decreases the inequality of income because more escape poverty by attaining employment and higher incomes. Yet, when the financial benefits gained from educational attainment decrease, fewer will seek more education. The result is an increase in the inequality of income as more people remain impoverished.

Becker reports that the other major factor in explaining the gap between the rich and the poor is the influence of the family "on knowledge, skills, health, values, and habits of their children. Parents affect educational attainment, marital stability, propensities to smoke, to get to work on time, and many other dimensions of their children's lives."[14]

The rising number of children born into single-parent households is strong evidence of the weakening of the family structure. According to Becker's research, this trend promotes greater inequality of income. More and more people remain poor. The gap widens if more people become rich, all else being the same, or if more people become poor, all else being the same.

Important Economic Principles: Economic Growth and the Plight of the Poor

Consider two paths by which the impoverished can obtain more of the necessities and luxuries of life. One path is through the attainment

---

14. The Concise Encyclopedia of Economics, s.v. "Human Capital," by Gary S. Becker, accessed August 2, 2014, http://www.econlib.org/library/Enc/Human Capital.html.

of higher earnings. The other is through income redistribution—government provision of food, housing, medical care, and cash. Both improve access to goods and services available in the marketplace. Some of our economists find that the paths have differing consequences.

We continue with recent studies of economic growth. Dollar and Kraay from the World Bank completed an important study in 2001 of ninety-two countries over the course of forty years of history. They found that through economic growth, people in the lowest 20 percent of the income distribution (the poor) on average experienced increased earnings and improved standards of living. On average, economic growth benefitted the rich and the poor proportionally. This is an important finding. This work, and the work of many others reporting similar results, argue that the promotion of economic growth is an effective, proven method of reducing the number of people living in poverty.

Ravallion, also of the World Bank, cautions the reader that what Dollar and Kraay reported is true, but the average does not always describe every country's experience. There are some countries in which economic growth did little for the poor. There are others where economic growth benefited the poor more than the rich. The former condition happens when the poor are isolated geographically and are not integrated into most of society. Surely there were times when Native Americans on reservations found little benefit from the economic growth taking place in the major industrial centers. Yet, the Dollar and Kraay results are compelling. Moreover, they found that the gains of the poor from economic growth were greater in countries with a *strong rule of law, active international trade, and developed financial markets.*

Ravallion's findings are important. There are instances in which economic growth did little for the poor. These are the exceptions, but they are nevertheless important. To help the poor the most, Ravallion advises us that economic growth must be of the type that creates employment opportunities for the poor. All economic growth is beneficial, but economic growth that increases the demand for unskilled labor is particularly beneficial to the poor. Ravallion cautioned against the adoption of any policies that focused upon reducing income inequality at the expense of economic growth.

In summary, our established economic principles are these:

- The value of a product is expressed by its price in a market-place and is governed by the interaction of demand and supply.

- Economic growth is effective in reducing the number of people in poverty.

- Economic growth is most effective when the form of growth increases employment among those in poverty.

- Economic growth is more likely when there is a rule of law, international trade, and a sufficient banking system.

- Economic growth is driven by entrepreneurial activity that requires risk taking, sufficient profits to justify risk taking, and access to loans necessary to fund new ventures.

- Entitlements to the poor can dissuade many from seeking improvement in education and skills and finding and keeping employment.

These economic principles are widely accepted and are supported with considerable research. The early understandings of economic principles, particularly in the twelfth and thirteenth centuries, affected Christian teachings and moral law. According to Telushkin, they actually inhibited economic development and growth—the very processes by which the poor benefit the most. Unfortunately, some of these misunderstandings continue to find their way into today's conversations. For example, the wages fund theory argues that increases in one's wage necessarily means others' wages must be reduced. The misunderstandings of established economic principles have not served us well. Those who most suffer from the consequences of these misunderstandings are the poor.

The next chapter introduces the religious doctrine of Judaism. Christianity has roots in Judaism, but it developed apart from some sacred religious writings that are integral to Judaism. Both Jesus and the Apostle Paul were well versed in Judaism, and it is within this context that some key biblical scriptures are reviewed in chapter 7.

Chapter 3

Early Judaism

Judaism also insists that man should develop a sense of responsibility for his world, including for the plight of the needy. It is this combination of honest labor and the giving of charity that mark the true fulfillment of man's divine nature.[1]

—Joseph Isaac Lifshitz

Although there are many religions of the world, our principal interest here is in the United States, where three religious groups dominate American society: Protestants, Catholics, and Jews. They are all related in important ways. Jewish theology formed the foundation for the Catholic faith, and Protestants emerged from the Catholic Church after Martin Luther posted his ninety-five edicts on the door of a church in Germany in 1517.

Summaries of doctrine from any of these three religious bodies should admit that there are controversies and debates over interpretations of scripture as well as other writings among their own religious leaders. The intent here is not to fairly disclose their differing beliefs or understandings. Instead, the intent is to recognize certain economic understandings that are similar among the three religious bodies. Some leaders within each of these do not support these understandings, but many do. The intention of this review is to highlight these common understandings insofar as they relate to views of the rich and the poor.

---

1. Joseph Isaac Lifshitz, *Judaism, Law & Free Markets: An Analysis* (Grand Rapids, MI: Acton Institute, 2012), 21.

The Development of the Jewish Sacred Scripture

The Old Testament of the Christian Bible is shared among the three religious groups. It begins with the Torah (the first five books of the Old Testament), which features speeches from Moses. The remainder of the Old Testament largely consists of wisdom writings (e.g., Proverbs), and a large portion of the Old Testament is devoted to the sayings of prophets. The Christian Bible, of course, contains the canonical Gospels (Matthew, Mark, Luke, and John), the letters of the Apostle Paul, Luke's Acts, and contributions of other writers. Thus, the Christian sacred scriptures contain materials not found within Jewish sacred scripture (e.g., the New Testament), and we find that Jewish sacred scriptures (e.g., the Mishnah) contain materials not found in Christian sacred scriptures. It is the latter that is of particular interest.

Some historians speculate that the exodus of the Israelites from Egypt took place around 1250 BCE. A firm date is not possible. Some scholars date the completion of the Old Testament around the third century BCE. Christ's ministry took place between 25 and 30 CE. The first Christians started meeting between 30 and 40 CE. The Apostle Paul's first letters were written between 50 and 59 CE. The first Gospel was probably written by Mark between 70 and 79 CE.[2] The Vulgate, the first Latin translation of the then complete Bible, was finished in 383 CE. Since 383 CE, there have been many releases of the Christian Bible—some more influential than others. These are important dates, albeit not exact, but close enough.

Important Historical Events

In 67 BCE when the Hellenistic Queen Shlomtzion Alexandra died, the Greek rulers, the Seleucids, over the lands in Palestine, struggled over who would be the next king, given that she bore two sons, the elder being of questionable abilities. Jewish factions split over the choice

---

2. M. J. Borg, *Evolution of the Word: New Testament in the Order the Books Were Written* (New York: HarperCollins, 2012).

between two sons—Hycranus II and Aristobulus.[3] Jewish leaders feared the development of widespread conflict, so the Romans were invited to occupy Judea to settle the controversy.[4] Some writers contend that the Romans invaded Judea, but other writers of history argue that the Romans were actually asked to occupy Judea to ensure peace.

Roman occupation continued through the birth, death, and resurrection of Christ and beyond. Early Christians were persecuted. The Roman emperor Nero authorized widespread killings of Christians between 64 and 68 CE—particularly after the fire in Rome in 64 CE, for which Nero blamed the Christians. During the time of the Christian persecutions, up until Constantine adopted Christianity as the official Byzantine religion in 313 CE, the Jews reportedly offered little assistance to the Christians and, at times, assisted the Romans in identifying Christians for persecution.[5]

Between 66 and 70 CE, groups of Jews engaged in riots against Roman rule and occupation. During this time a small army of Jews successfully drove the Roman garrison out of Jerusalem. In response, Rome sent an army of sixty thousand Roman soldiers into the northern territories of Galilee, killing or enslaving one hundred thousand Jews. Many fled as refugees to Jerusalem.

During this time, a growing Jewish political group, called Zealots, organized and sought to unify the Jews in open rebellion against the Romans. Their methods were ruthless—killing Romans and Jewish sympathizers. A civil war erupted. One million Jews lost their lives during this civil war—most at the hands of Jews.[6] The Romans destroyed the second temple in Jerusalem in 70 CE.

Some sixty years later the Bar-Kokhba Rebellion began in response to harsh Roman restrictions imposed upon the Jews, including making circumcision and reading the Torah capital offenses. This second rebellion led to the deaths of 50 percent of the population of Judea. By the end of this rebellion, non-Jews outnumbered the Jews in Judea. The Roman targets for execution included the rabbis and the priests.

---

3. Rabbi Joseph Telushkin, *Jewish Literacy* (New York: HarperCollins, 1991), 119.

4. Ibid., 36.

5. Ibid., 37.

6. Ibid., 38.

Judaism and the Oral Law

Our review of early Judaism begins with the Torah, Genesis through Deuteronomy—the first five books in the Christian Bible and the Hebrew Bible. The Torah is the foundation of Jewish law and is viewed as superior to all other scripture. In Orthodox Judaism, the Torah is of divine origin, being handed down from God to Moses at Mount Sinai. The remainder of the Hebrew Bible does not have the significance or the authority of the Torah.[7]

The book of Exodus explains the history of Moses's visits to Mount Sinai, where he received the stone tablets containing the Ten Commandments. Recall that Moses broke the first set of tablets in anger and returned to Mount Sinai. According to tradition, Moses received the additional laws from God, some recorded in the Torah and others retained as Judaism's oral law.[8]

For several centuries, the Jews chose not to retain the oral law in written form. Instead, they preferred that it be taught by rabbis and priests. The teaching of the oral law gave the temple an additional important function in Jewish society—the place where Jews learned the rest of what God revealed to Moses on Mount Sinai. It elevated the importance of the rabbis and priests in the Jewish communities. It emphasized the importance of communications between and among generations—creating an additional purpose for a strong family unit.

The oral law remains an important source of Jewish understandings. According to Tamari, "the revelation at Sinai included an oral law—or, more correctly, oral tradition. This *Torah She Be'al Peh* (oral law) was (according to Judaism) given to Moses as well, so that the two, the oral and the written law, form one unit; Jewish law cannot be conceived of, let alone applied, without reference to this unity."[9]

---

7. This point is disputed among Jewish scholars.

8. Telushkin, *Jewish Literacy*, 149. "Orthodox Judaism claims that most of the oral traditions recorded in these books [Mishnah and Talmud] dates back to God's revelation to Moses on Mount Sinai. When God gave Moses the Torah, Orthodoxy teaches, He simultaneously transmitted that Oral Law to his successor, Joshua, who transmitted it to his successor, in a chain that is still carried on."

9. Ibid., 12.

To a large extent, the oral law serves as the "interpreter's Bible," providing additional material to explain the written words in the Old Testament. Several examples demonstrate this point.

The Old Testament text, often quoted, demands an eye for an eye, a tooth for a tooth as a matter of justice.[10] Oral tradition in the Mishnah makes it clear that justice does not require that the eye of the guilty party be destroyed but that the monetary value of an eye be paid by the guilty party to the victim.[11] Thus, oral law provides additional instruction.

The Ten Commandments declare that one should not kill. The Mishnah explains that the commandment refers to murder—not all killing. In fact, the oral law requires one to kill an intruder in self-defense before being killed.[12] Oral law provides the additional instruction.

With the substantial loss of rabbis and priests through the two rebellions, Jewish leaders feared for the preservation of oral law. In a break from tradition, oral law had to be recorded. Rabbi Judah the Prince is credited with the written form of the Mishnah in 200 CE.[13] Around 400 CE the Talmud was constructed, containing the Mishnah and commentaries on the oral Torah. Christianity and its sacred scriptures were being compiled before the Mishnah was completed—a potentially important sequence of events.[14]

---

10. Exod 21:24.

11. Mishnah, *Bava Kamma* 8:1, eMishnah, 2008, http://www.emishnah.com/PDFs/Bava%20Kamma%208.pdf. "One who injures a fellow man becomes liable to him for five items: for depreciation, for pain, for healing, for loss of time, and for degradation. How so regarding depreciation? If he put out his eye, cut off his arm, or broke his leg, the injured person is considered as though he were a [Hebrew] slave, being sold in the marketplace... and a valuation is made as to how much he is worth [previously, before the injury], and how much he is worth [now]."

12. Mishnah, *Sanhedrin* 8:6, eMishnah, 2008, http://www.emishnah.com/PDFs/Sanhedrin%208.pdf. "[The thief] who tunnels his way [into a house may be killed by the owner of the house and] is judged on account of his eventual outcome [since he will most likely murder the owner of the house, if he encounters him.]"

13. Telushkin, *Jewish Literacy*, 150.

14. St. Athanasius of Alexandria is credited for the listing of the books that formed the Christian canon around 325 CE. This suggests that New Testament writers had access to the Mishnah, which contradicts the notion that these Jewish teachings were not available by the accident of time.

Recall that Paul's letters were written between 50 and 59 CE. The book of Mark was written between 70 and 79 CE, and other Gospels were written shortly thereafter. Rabbi Judah the Prince completed the Mishnah around 200 CE. Thus, only Jews well versed in oral law could have provided the writers of the New Testament, particularly the writers of the Gospels, the sacred messages that had not yet been recorded.

The Apostle Paul, of course, was one exception, being an author of New Testament scripture and well versed in oral law. Paul's letters emphasize the unmerited grace of God as the means of salvation through Jesus's faithfulness on the cross. He rejected righteousness by following the law but accepted righteousness by faith in Christ.[15] Paul's letters do not condemn oral law as instructions for righteous living. Paul's letters make it clear that adherence to the law is insufficient for salvation.

Perhaps due to the absence of Mishnah during the first century or the religious separation between Christians and Jews, the early Christian church did not recognize the Mishnah or the Talmud as a strict sacred interpretation of the Torah. Christian scholars, unlike the Jewish scholars, do not routinely turn to the Mishnah or the Talmud to help with interpretations of scripture.

Christians understand that Jesus and the Apostle Paul were each Jews well educated in Jewish doctrine. According to scripture, the Apostle Paul was taught by one of the most revered rabbis in history—Gamaliel.[16] The Mishnah notes that Gamaliel was one of the greatest teachers in all the annals of Judaism. The Talmud reports that Gamaliel was president of the Great Sanhedrin in Jerusalem—the highest court in the land.

Jesus and the Apostle Paul each had a strong grasp of oral law, which continued to evolve until the fourth century CE. Thus, in reading the Gospels and the letters of the Apostle Paul, it is useful to remember these facts. Jewish doctrine, expressed in the Mishnah and the Talmud, can be helpful in considering the plight of the rich and the poor in Jesus's teachings and the Apostle Paul's letters.[17]

---

15. Gal 3:11.

16. Acts 22:3.

17. There is a long history of debates concerning the usefulness of the Talmud among Christian scholars. Reportedly, the first recorded public burnings of the Talmud occurred in France in 1242. Hyam Maccoby in *Judaism on Trial: Jewish-*

Essential Jewish Perspectives

Jewish oral traditions strongly underscore two biblical teachings in Genesis: the earth and its contents are a gift from God to be used for human benefit, and humans are made in the image of God. According to some interpretation of scripture, the human is to have dominion over the earth for the human's personal pleasure. Meir Tamari notes that compensation for one's labor and the resulting accumulation of possessions are both consistent with God's intent. Biblical scripture leads to the understanding that if one observes the commandments, one will accumulate wealth. The accumulation of wealth is not an unearned blessing from God.[18]

The Torah does not glorify poverty, and there are no vows of poverty in rabbinic Judaism that would place the poor man in the more blessed state. The Talmud exhorts the principles of property rights—the rule of law. There is a strong prohibition against theft—taking of one's property. "Theft constitutes a double crime, as it were, against one's fellow man and against God, who forbade it."[19]

According to Genesis, God made the human in God's own image:

> Then God said, "Let us make humanity in our image to resemble us so that
> they may take charge of the fish of the sea, the birds of the sky, the livestock,
> all the earth, and all the crawling things on earth."
> God created humanity in God's own image,
> in the divine image God created them,
> male and female God created them.[20]

Since God created the heavens and the earth, and humans were made in God's image, humans, therefore, must also create.[21] God did not finish creation but left all remaining creation tasks to us. We are

---

Christian Disputations in the Middle Ages, (Madison, NJ: Fairleigh Dickinson University Press, 1981).

18. Meir Tamari, *With All Your Possessions: Jewish Ethics and Economic Life*, Kupietzky ed. (Jerusalem: Maggid Books, 1998), 29.

19. Ibid., 42–43.

20. Gen 1:26-27.

21. Throughout these chapters, there are general references to "man" and "his," which have for centuries referred to humankind.

to bring creation to a higher level of completion. This teaching, contained in the Talmud, imposes upon humans the obligation to express dominion over the material world and to continue God's completion of creation. God assigns these obligations to us.

The remaining tasks of creation are then manifested in one's chosen trade or profession. This is the essence of the work ethic. We dedicate ourselves to our work. We find solace in our work and in so doing are obedient to God. According to Jewish law, this is our religious calling.

The ability to create depends in part upon one's understanding of the world and humanity. This is enhanced with education, training, and experience. Thus, one can better fulfill one's obligation to create by better preparation through effort and dedication. Obviously, a strong work ethic is a critical component of one's character, which is a reflection of God.

Conditions are placed upon the observant Jewish in accumulating wealth. It is important to discern *how* the Jewish person accumulates wealth. According to Corinne and Robert Sauer, a worker "is obligated to participate in the creative process, should not be demotivated by inadequate protection of private property, and is blessed when the outcome of honest labor is the accumulation of wealth."[22] An emphasis on honesty is not to be taken lightly.

The *Mishnah Torah*, consisting of fourteen volumes, was written by Maimonides between 1170 and 1180 CE, and is considered a complete statement of oral law. Maimonides was a Jewish rabbi in Egypt, and is viewed as one of the most influential Torah scholars in Jewish history. He wrote of the Torah scholar: "His commerce shall be conducted in truth and faith. His word shall be his bond, and he shall be scrupulous in his accounting. He shall always be ready to concede to others when he buys from them and should not press his interests on them."[23] The righteous Jew is to become a scholar of the Torah, spending considerable time in study. This necessarily limits one's time available for economic activities. The Torah scholar has little time to waste.

The accumulation of wealth, when achieved honestly, reflects the fortunate consequence of dedicated work and effort as well as a chosen craft or profession that is rewarded handsomely in the marketplace.

---

22. Corinne Sauer and Robert M. Sauer, *Judaism, Markets, and Capitalism* (Grand Rapids, MI: Acton Institute, 2006),14–15.

23. Tamari, *With All Your Possessions*, quoting the *Mishnah Torah*, 62.

Economics tells us that the wages of labor differ according to the market value of what labor produces. The wages of a carpenter's helper will usually be less than that of the carpenter—the latter being more highly skilled and therefore scarce. Competition for carpenters' services typically drives these wages upward when construction activities in the community expand and only a few carpenters are around. Most anyone can be quickly trained to become a carpenter's helper, so the large pool of those seeking employment as a carpenter's helper keeps these wages at the lower levels. Economic forces at work drive these results. Judaism does not quarrel with the inequality of these two levels of wages.

Joseph Lifshitz writes: "Judaism holds a fundamentally positive view of individual wealth. Property is an expression of man's sovereignty, his capacity to rule over the material world, so that he may benefit from it, care for it, and perfect it through creative acts. It is the most apparent means through which 'God's image' is expressed in human life."[24]

Thus, Judaism holds no particular disfavor toward the higher-income individuals if the higher income is attained honestly. Nor does Judaism hold any disfavor for the individuals who heavily invest in education and training, thereby acquiring the skills and education that are more highly rewarded in the marketplace. With such skills and education, the capacity to create improves. Thus, those acquiring the more valued skills and education are being obedient to God's calling. Meir Tamari concludes that the scriptures require no vow of poverty as one seeks salvation.[25]

Jewish workers who attain financial success are not to publicly demonstrate their achievements through fashion and dress. According to Maimonides, the Torah scholar is to provide for his family without excessive accumulation of property. The scholar is to stand out from others through his wisdom, piety, and appropriate actions. He should not dress as kings nor as those in poverty. His clothing should appear ordinary.[26] Flaunting one's wealth is to be avoided.

Judaism is not silent on the appropriate use of accumulated wealth. According to Lifshitz, "Judaism also insists that man should develop a sense of responsibility for his world, including for the plight of the

---

24. Joseph Isaac Lifshitz, *Judaism, Law & the Free Market: An Analysis* (Grand Rapids, MI: Acton Institute, 2012), 21.
25. Tamari, *With All Your Possessions,* 30.
26. Tamari, *With All Your Possessions,* quoting *Mishnah Torah,* 59–60.

needy. It is this combination of honest labor and the giving of charity that mark the true fulfillment of man's divine nature."[27]

Jews are to assume responsibility for the needy. They face the moral obligation to share with others. Yet, there are priorities in sharing with the needy.

The giver, who has acquired the wealth which is to be shared, owns the right to select those who are to receive. That is, there is an obligation to share, but no one else has the authority to determine who is to benefit from this charity.[28]

Judaism provides listing of priorities. Members of the family come first. This confirms the importance of family in the Jewish faith. One must seek to prevent another from falling into poverty—especially family members.

Members of one's own community come second. Presumably these are neighbors and friends who find themselves in need. Since the individual Jew owns the right to select who is to receive, it is reasonable to believe that the giver personally knows the individuals in the community in need. Since charity is not under the control and authority of anyone else, the giver is in control.

Others, after family and members of the community, come third. Presumably, these recipients are identified by others who personally know of those in need beyond one's community. Those directing these charities could be the rabbi or priest. It could be a Jewish charity organized for a specific cause. Whatever the need, it comes only after one's family and members of one's community are considered.

Judaism holds a strong quest for support of the common good. To support the common good, it is appropriate to enact taxes in order to finance favored public projects. Several taxing principles have been adopted, including per capita taxes, individual benefit taxes, and taxes

---

27. Joseph Isaac Lifshitz, *Judaism, Law & the Free Market: An Analysis* (Grand Rapids, MI: Acton Institute, 2012), 21.

28. Ibid., 18. "In Judaism, the idea of charity focuses on the donor and his relationship with the poor, not on the recipient. Its aim is to cultivate a sense of responsibility, as a moral and religious obligation. For this reason, the rabbis maintained that the donor should favor his relatives over strangers.... By giving to those for whom he feels a special obligation, the donor expresses his self-understanding as a unique individual who takes responsibility for those around him."

proportional to one's wealth. Income taxes are a more modern extension of taxation.

Within Jewish scriptures, there appears to be no reference to taxes imposed for redistribution of wealth or income. This follows from the respect for the entrepreneur or laborer who is diligent and dedicated to the chosen tasks. Meir Tamari reports that, in constrast to the glorification of poverty among some faiths and creeds, Judaism views the accumulation of wealth as desirable.[29] Moreover, there is no desire to establish a formal system for redistribution of wealth in spite of the Jewish law requiring provisions and assistance to those in need. Judaism is concerned with the negative impact of charity upon the recipient and the establishment of welfare as a right rather than a privilege.[30]

The clear responsibility of those with means is to care for the poor. This responsibility cannot be missed in even casual reading of Jewish scriptures. Yet, the provision of welfare to the poor must preserve the honor and dignity of those being served. They must not be insulted or slighted. According to Maimonides, the preferred form of support for a Jew who has become poor is a gift, a loan, or employment. The objective is to break out of the poverty cycle. This is the highest degree of charity.[31] These Jewish beliefs have parallel examples in Christian doctrine adopted as guidelines for the provision of charity to the poor in early America, as will be presented in later chapters.

Jewish sacred authorities include the Hebrew Bible, the Mishnah, and the Talmud—the latter two sources reflecting oral traditions passed on since the time of Moses on Mount Sinai. The writings of the books of the New Testament took place before the Mishnah and the Talmud were completed. Perhaps due to the accident of timing or the division between Jews and Christians over essential Christian doctrine, early Christians did not consider writings contained in the Mishnah nor the Talmud as sacred scripture. Accordingly, Judaism includes doctrine that is not often recognized within Christian literature. Some teachings in Christianity find parallels to the following teachings that appear to emerge from Judaism, according to Lifshitz:

---

29. Tamari, *With All Your Possessions*, 30.
30. Ibid., 268.
31. Ibid., 273.

- Man was created to continue God's creation through his own work.[32]

- Man is obligated to create, using the best of his skills and education, and diligence.[33]

- The honest accumulation of wealth occurs as a result of righteous living and following God's laws.[34]

- Man is to avoid becoming dependent upon the income of others.[35]

- Man is to share his wealth with others: family first, friends and neighbors second, and others third.[36]

- The greatest form of charity is helping one to remain financially independent of others.[37]

- Man must respect the property rights of others—the rule of law.[38]

- Redistribution of income as a public policy is a foreign concept.[39]

These components of Jewish teaching were circulating when Jesus and the Apostle Paul were engaged in their ministries. As considered in the next chapter, this is the context within which Christ's teachings and the crafting of Paul's letters are housed.

---

32. Lifshitz, *Judaism, Law & the Free Market,* 11; Tamari, *With All Your Possessions,* 29.

33. Tamari, *With All Your Possessions,* 29.

34. Lifshitz, *Judaism, Law & the Free Market,* 21.

35. Lifshitz, *Judaism, Law, & the Free Market,* 15; Tamari, *With All Your Possessions,* 298.

36. Lifshitz, *Judaism, Law, & the Free Market,* 18, 39, 72.

37. Ibid., 71.

38. Ibid., 13.

39. Lifshitz, *Judaism, Law, & the Free Market,* 54; Tamari, *With All Your Possessions,* 267–68.

Chapter 4

Jesus Christ and the Apostle Paul

"Don't even begin to think that I have come to do away with the Law and the Prophets. I haven't come to do away with them but to fulfill them. I say to you very seriously that as long as heaven and earth exist, neither the smallest letter nor even the smallest stroke of a pen will be erased from the Law until everything there becomes a reality."
—Matthew 5:17-18

Within the Jewish community of Israel, Jesus of Nazareth was born; raised by his parents, Joseph and Mary; taught the sacred scriptures of Judaism and the oral law; became an adult; learned the trade of a carpenter; and by the age of thirty began his three-year ministry that forever changed the world.

His teachings during his three-year ministry are captured in the New Testament—mostly found in the canonical Gospels of Matthew, Mark, Luke, and John. The meanings of his life and ministry are presented and explained in the letters of the Apostle Paul and in the other remaining books of the New Testament.

Most would agree that writings about Jesus's life and teachings, coupled with Paul's letters, have largely formed Christian doctrine over the centuries. The accumulated Christian literature from the first century until modern times devotes a considerable focus upon these two individuals. Since many of the quoted scriptures concerning the rich

39

and the poor come from Jesus's teachings and Paul's letters, it is useful to consider their lives as Jews, participating in economies of their day.

Jesus of Nazareth

As an adult and before his ministry began, Jesus was a tradesman—a carpenter presumably trained by his father, Joseph.[1] Little is known about his work and life as a carpenter, but understandings from economic history and archeological findings help fill this void. What follows is a reasonable portrait of Jesus's adult life before his ministry.

During these times, Nazareth was a small town in the midst of Roman-occupied territory. Within an hour's walk of Nazareth, the Romans were rebuilding the city of Sepphoris. This city had been destroyed by Roman legions in response to riots and rebellions following the death of Herod the Great. Herod Antipas, the assigned ruler of Galilee and Peraea as prescribed in Herod the Great's will, selected Sepphoris as his regional capital in 3 BCE, about the time of Jesus's birth. The reconstruction of Sepphoris continued throughout Jesus's life as a carpenter.

There remains little of the city today, so our knowledge is based largely upon archeological excavations and what fragments of written history remain.[2] The excavations that began in 1980 were led by James F. Strange, along with Richard A. Bately. After six years of excavation, many of the details of the old city were revealed. These findings, along with the history recorded by Josephus, who resided in Sepphoris, potentially change the present understanding of Jesus's practice of his craft.

Sepphoris developed into a modern city of thirty thousand residents—a city of sophisticated inhabitants including Jews, Arabs, Greeks, and Romans. In comparison, Jerusalem's population was eighty thousand. The theatre at Sepphoris could seat four thousand and was reportedly a common place for Roman drama.

---

1. Jesus is identified as a carpenter in Mark 6:3. The original Greek word used in this verse, *tektōn*, more generally means "artisan" and can be applied to woodworkers, stonemasons, and blacksmiths. See Richard A. Batey, *Jesus and the Forgotten City: New Light on Sepphoris and the Urban World of Jesus* (New York: Baker Book House, 1991), 76.

2. Batey, *Jesus and the Forgotten City.*

Archeological findings and economic history help paint a portrait of Jesus the carpenter that is perhaps different from what most have been led to believe—a young man in a small wood shop in Nazareth. The considerable reconstruction of Sepphoris required large numbers of skilled craftsmen, including carpenters. Such a massive undertaking would attract carpenters from neighboring towns, such as Nazareth, to meet the demands for skilled craftsmen. It is highly likely that Jesus would have been directly affected by this growing demand. Even if Jesus chose not to work in Sepphoris, the value of his skills would have been increased anyway as contractors of the day searched for more and more skilled craftsmen.

This is the puzzle faced by those who seek to accurately describe the life of Jesus, as an adult, before he began his ministry. This is important because this portrait of Jesus as a carpenter helps in understanding Jesus's parables and his teachings. This portrait of Jesus, working as an artisan in the reconstruction of Sepphoris, is strikingly different from the portrait of a simple woodworker, working in a small shop in a small, rural village—a portrait I had formed from my earliest days in Sunday school. My previous vision of Jesus, the carpenter, assigned Jesus to the lower-income classes because of the lack of economic opportunities and an unsubstantiated view of a young man spending much of his time reading and studying scripture.

Consider a more informed view of Jesus the carpenter. His parents were Jews obedient to Jewish Law—both written and oral. Luke 2:41 says of Joseph and Mary: "Each year his parents went to Jerusalem for the Passover Festival." It is reasonable to conclude that Jesus' earthly parents hoped for him to grow to become a righteous Jew, following the dictates of Jewish Law.

Among the teachings of Judaism pertinent to this line of reasoning is the duty of the individual to work so that one does not become economically dependent upon another. According to Joseph Lifshitz, "Jewish law calls on man to do everything in his power to avoid becoming dependent upon his community for his welfare."[3] Corinne Sauer and Robert M. Sauer quote the famous Rabbi Maimonides: "whomsoever has in his heart that he shall indulge in the study of the Torah and do

---

3. Lifshitz, *Judaism, Law, & the Free Market*, 15.

no work but rather be sustained from charity, defames the Lord's name, cheapens the Torah, extinguishes the light of faith, causes himself ill and removes himself from the world to come."[4]

This principle is made quite clear in a teaching from the Talmud, reported by Meir Tamari:

> "For over a dozen years, it is taught, Shimon Bar Yohai hid in a cave studying the Torah, despite a Roman edict against it. On leaving the cave he saw a man plowing a field. 'What!' he said. 'There is so little time to devote oneself to God's words, and you devote your time to insignificant things like the settlement of the world.' And in his anger he turned the man into a heap of bones. This incident was repeated when he came across another person engaged in farming activities. Then a heavenly voice said to him: 'Bar Yohai, unless you refrain from turning My world into chaos, I will put you back in the cave."[5]

Elsewhere it is said that one should work on the Sabbath if it is necessary to avoid financial dependence upon others.[6] It is perhaps misdirected to imagine Jesus as a carpenter who ignored the economic opportunities that developed and instead remained a full-time student of the Torah, allowing family and friends to provide for his subsistence.

In his ministry, after his years as a carpenter, Matthew records him saying:

> "Don't even begin to think that I have come to do away with the Law and the Prophets. I haven't come to do away with them but to fulfill them. I say to you very seriously that as long as heaven and earth exist, neither the smallest letter nor even the smallest stroke of a pen will be erased from the Law until everything there becomes a reality."[7]

Jesus understood Jewish written and oral law, including the obligation to earn an income and remain independent of others for financial sup-

---

4. Corinne Sauer and Robert M. Sauer, *Judaism, Markets, and Capitalism* (Grand Rapids, MI: Acton Institute, 2006), 15. To be sure, Maimonides was a scholar of the twelfth century but was a student of the Talmud.

5. Meir Tamari, *With All Your Possessions, 27.*

6. As reported in Lifshitz, *Judaism, Law, & the Free Market*, 15: "It is better to profane your Sabbath than to become dependent upon others.

7. Matt 5:17-19.

port. Jesus probably took advantage of the economic opportunities that developed for artisans of his caliber.

The fact that Sepphoris was being reconstructed during Jesus's adult life means that his earnings could have been well above that of unskilled laborers. Jesus would not have been poor by the standards of the day. Moreover, Jesus would have been exposed to the elite, including those associated with the theatre, higher governmental offices, and the richer entrepreneurs. In speaking of the rich man during his ministry, it is likely that he had seen such men many times in Sepphoris. He would have observed the impact of nearby economic growth and its impact upon the smaller town of Nazareth. He would have observed the industries of the entrepreneurs and the business risks they faced, given that many might have been the clients employing the work of carpenters. Jesus did not grow up in a small village surrounded by agricultural-based businesses with little differences in resident incomes. Instead, Jesus was exposed to the most advanced urban commerce in the region and was well aware of the substantial gap between the rich and the poor.

As a Jew, Jesus would have understood the expectation that one should never live off the income of others. As a skilled carpenter in the shadows of Sepphoris, he may have had ample opportunity to earn sufficient income to remain financially independent until he began his ministry. During his earning years, he would have likely lived at the upper-income categories of a skilled tradesman. It is unlikely that Jesus was poor during his adult life.[8]

It is useful to contrast his adult life before and during his ministry. Before his ministry, he was a craftsman capable of earning an income sufficient to remaining financially independent. No written history proves that he was anything else. His ministry required teaching, preaching, and travel. There are few, if any, accounts that he continued his work as a craftsman during his ministry. He appears to have made a complete, perhaps rapid, transition from craftsman to one fully engaged in ministry. Accordingly, Jesus likely relied upon the generosities of others to support his needs for food, clothing, and shelter during his ministry.

---

8. Some scriptures suggest that, once in full-time ministry, depending upon gifts from others is preferable (e.g., Matt 10:9 and Matt 19:21).

From an economic perspective, receiving support from others to support his ministry is not being financially dependent. Instead, it is receiving support from those who value his ministry—a ministry business model that prevails even today. It is not surprising that Jesus sent his twelve disciples to begin their ministries without "gold or silver or copper for [their] money belts to take on [their] trips...a backpack for the road or two shirts or sandals or a walking stick."[9] Each was to receive support from those receiving the message. This is not financial dependence.

The Apostle Paul

The Apostle Paul was a well-educated Pharisee and a tentmaker. His native city was Cilicia, which was known to export cloth made of goat's hair. He was educated in Jewish law by Gamaliel, who was an outstanding teacher. Gamaliel served as president of the Great Sanhedrin in Jerusalem—perhaps equivalent to the chief justice of the Supreme Court in our times. Paul was a true scholar of Jewish law.

He joined Aquila and Priscilla, both also tentmakers, in a business venture.[10] The Gospels report that Paul spent considerable time making tents in order to support himself and his ministries. He, too, was a skilled craftsman. As a well-educated Jew, he would not have sought the financial support of others unless he was providing services of some kind.

The Gospels report that Paul received some level of financial support from churches that he founded.

> Did I commit a sin by humbling myself to give you an advantage because I preached the gospel of God to you free of charge? I robbed other churches by taking a salary from them in order to serve you! While I was with you, I didn't burden any of you even though I needed things. The believers who came from Macedonia gave me everything I needed. I kept myself from being a financial drain on you in any way, and I will continue to keep myself from being a burden.[11]

---

9. Matt 10:9-10.
10. Acts 18:1-3.
11. 2 Cor 11:7-9.

It seems that Paul regretted receiving funds from the other churches for his work with the Corinthian churches. Yet the scriptures are clear that he worked in the cities in which he preached in support of his necessities and conveniences.

As a tentmaker, one would likely find the best markets for his products on the trade routes where potential customers were traveling from and to distant places. Major trade routes at that time included Athens, Corinth, Collossae, Philippi, and Thessalonika. Whether by design or by circumstance, Paul was often positioned to benefit from strong demands for the products of his labor.

Paul, as an obedient Jew, provided valuable instruction to the Thessalonians:

> Brothers and sisters, we command you in the name of our Lord Jesus Christ to stay away from every brother or sister who lives an undisciplined life that is not in line with the traditions that you received from us. You yourselves know how you need to imitate us because we were not undisciplined when we were with you. We didn't eat anyone's food without paying for it. Instead, we worked night and day with effort and hard work so that we would not impose on you. We did this to give you an example to imitate, not because we didn't have a right to insist on financial support. Even when we were with you we were giving you this command: "If anyone doesn't want to work, they shouldn't eat." We hear that some of you are living an undisciplined life. They aren't working, but they are meddling in other people's business. By the Lord Jesus Christ, we command and encourage such people to work quietly and put their own food on the table. Brothers and sisters, don't get discouraged in doing what is right.[12]

Note the reference to the tradition Paul taught the Thessalonians—avoid idleness. Consider the reference to the avoidance of eating another's bread without paying for it. Remember the reference to Christ's teaching that one should earn his or her own living. Paul understood the Jewish prohibition against financial dependence upon others.

As with Jesus, Paul depended in part upon the generosities from those he served. As noted, he was hesitant to depend upon these generosities. Nevertheless, Paul worked at times as a tent maker during his years of ministry. The financial support he received from others appears to have come from those he served—similar to the model employed by

---

12. 2 Thess 3:6-13.

Jesus and his disciples (i.e., receiving donations in return for the ministries provided).

Overview

The major points from this brief review of scripture and Roman history include the following possibilities:

- Both Jesus and Paul were well-educated Jews.

- Both sought to remain obedient to written and oral Jewish Law.

- Both understood the teaching that one must earn sufficient income so that one does not become dependent upon others.

- Both had opportunities as craftsmen to avoid poverty and to remain financially independent prior to their ministries.

- Neither appeared to take a vow of poverty as a demonstration of a sense of holiness or righteousness.

- Both received financial support from those they served in ministry.

- Neither became idle, becoming financially dependent upon others.

Chapter 5
Roman Catholicism

The fundamental principle about the significance and dignity of human work is this: "Human work proceeds directly from persons created in the image of God and called to prolong the work of creation."[1]
— Peter J. Kreeft

According to Catholic belief, the Catholic Church was founded by Christ, who passed its authority on to his apostles, who, in turn, turned it over to the bishops. Christ appointed the Apostle Peter as the head of the bishops—commonly referred to as the pope.[2] Over its two-thousand-year history, the Catholic Church has elected more than 260 popes. One might contend that this is sufficient time for countless theological inquiries and for Catholic doctrine to be well developed and clear. However, there have been differing opinions, even among the popes, in treatments of the inequality of income, the rich, and the poor.

The Protestant denominations have their roots in the Catholic faith, and inquiry into these roots is informative. Our principal interest is in tracing its religious perspectives on the rich and the inequality of income. Catholicism reflects some important departures from Judaism but also some common threads. Much of the Catholic doctrine relevant to our inquiry was influenced by major changes in governments, control of businesses, and restrictions on personal freedoms.

---

1. Peter J. Kreeft, *Catholic Christianity* (Chicago: Ignatius Press, 2001), 264.
2. Ibid., 98–100.

The following material first reviews the more general Catholic doctrine that considers the nature of man, demonstrating that it is similar to that of Judaism. Next we will examine Catholic understandings of capitalism and socialism, followed by views of the wealthy, vows of poverty, and salvation. Finally, the material presents two important papal letters that directly address the government's role in redistributing income from the rich to the poor.

The Nature of Humanity

Catholics believe in the dignity of the human. Only humans are created to know and love their creator—which sets them apart from all other living things. The human was created in the image of God and was given dominion over the earth: "man is superior to nature by his reason and free will..."[3] Man, the artist, is to use the elements of nature as his materials as well as his studio. Nature is to be understood, loved, and respected.

The implication seems consistent with the Jewish doctrine that humans are to continue the work of God's creation. The "artist" is one who is engaged in the work of a craft. Perhaps influenced by the Old Testament and early Judaism, Catholicism shares the view that a human is to engage in work. Such work is to continue the work of creation as a reflection of the human being made in the image of God. There is to be significance and dignity in human work.[4]

Catholicism also addresses the toil and unpleasantness of some work. Work is a consequence of the Fall. It can be punishing, but it shall be endured, in union with Christ who was crucified. There is a redemptive feature to punishing work since work can be a work of God. Of course, not all work is unpleasant.[5]

These materials do little to reflect the explanations from the economists; that is, work is a means for earning income by which market goods and services can be purchased. Thus far, there is nothing that

---

3. Ibid., 62.
4. Ibid., 264.
5. Ibid.

48

suggests work shall not lead to an unequal distribution of income—a disparity between the rich and the poor.

Within Catholic doctrine, all are called upon to extend charity to the poor. This is especially true for the rich. The attainment of wealth is not sinful. "Riches are not evil, nor are all rich people selfish. But riches are dangerous—more dangerous than we think, if we are to take Christ's repeated warnings seriously."[6]

Riches can become addictive, making generosity for some of the rich very difficult. Yet, we are called to share our riches with the poor.

Catholic doctrine encourages detachment from riches, since "The precept of detachment from riches is obligatory for entrance into the Kingdom of heaven."[7] Detachment from riches is liberating. It is based upon Luke 14:33: "In the same way, none of you who are unwilling to give up all of your possessions can be my disciple."

Thus, riches are not evil, but detachment from riches brings one closer to God. Although this seems to suggest a vow of poverty for all, the vow of poverty is fundamental only to religious orders.

Catholic doctrine stresses faith in Jesus Christ as a requirement for salvation. This, of course, is its central departure from Judaism. In contrast from most Protestants, salvation, according to Catholic doctrine, also requires good works. According to Catholic doctrine, good works are essential—a requirement for salvation. This division, between Protestant and Catholic, was the central issue during the Reformation and remains a "tragic division in the history of the Church."[8]

The requirement for good works obviously applies to both rich and poor. It seems logical that the rich, with substantially more resources at hand compared to the poor, would be required to do more than the poor in pursuit of salvation.

Modern descriptions of Catholic doctrine recognize the two major economic systems of the world—capitalism and socialism. These additions to Catholic doctrine came after the Industrial Revolution when societies began moving away from agriculture-dominated economies into industry-dominated economies. This new doctrine cautions against the

---

6. Ibid., 265.
7. Ibid., 267.
8. Ibid., 25.

implementation of extreme versions of either economic system—"hard" capitalism or "hard" socialism.[9]

Catholic doctrine expresses concern for any system in which economic forces guide or control all social relationships. Not all socialist governments are necessarily immoral by intent, but there remains a unique danger within societies based upon socialism. Within socialism, societies substitute collective organization for the basic rights of individuals, thereby depressing human dignity. Catholic doctrine has rejected modern expressions of socialism based upon totalitarian or atheistic ideologies, such as communism."[10]
At the other extreme, Catholic doctrine explains:

> The Church does not reject capitalism as such either. But "she has...refused to accept, in the practice of capitalism, individualism and the absolute primacy of the law of the marketplace over human labor.... [Capitalism that] makes profit the exclusive norm and ultimate end of economic activity is morally unacceptable....And the profit motive—a necessary virtue in capitalism—is often only another name for a capital vice, one of the "seven deadly sins," namely greed, or avarice.[11]

Catholic doctrine, however, recognizes the importance of the profit motive: "Profits are necessary, however. They make possible the investments that ensure the future of a business and they guarantee employment.... Profit is to production what pleasure is to sex: right and proper and natural when associated with the intrinsic purpose of the activity, but all too easily divorced from that purpose and loved for its own sake."[12]

It is common for economists to conclude that religious writers do not always have a firm grasp of economic theory just as religious writers contend that economists do not have a firm grasp of theology or religious history. Nevertheless, Catholic doctrine seems far too focused upon the sins of greed and less focused upon the routine operations of relatively free markets. Too often religious writers, as well as most others, begin with their own notions of the dominance

9. Ibid., 263.
10. Ibid., 263.
11. Ibid., 264.
12. Ibid., 264.

of the profit motive (a.k.a., greed) and illustrations of "champions" of capitalism who presumably built their empires off the backs of under-paid labor or child labor.

In discussing the great industrialists who built their factories, rail-roads, and oil refineries, Novak writes:

> Such industrial and commercial pioneers often took great pleasure in their creativity; they regarded themselves as artists, prided themselves on their intuitions and hunches, and gloried in the beauty of many of the things they produced. This was true not only of the first movie moguls and the founders of great newspapers, but also of those who built factories—or whole new industries—and skyscrapers, and airplanes, and so on. These romantics had the misfortune, however, to enter upon the world's stage at a moment when many European intellectuals were preaching pernicious doctrines quite hostile to the actual capitalist spirit.[13]

Many successful in business dedicate substantial amounts of time and energy to their work—not because of the quest for more money but because they love what they are doing. The accumulation of wealth is a welcomed by-product of their activities.

Catholic doctrine accepts the traditional seven deadly sins, one of which is gluttony—the quest for an "inordinate amount of worldly goods."[14] Peter Kreeft quotes from the *Catechism of the Catholic Church*: "Human work proceeds directly from persons created in the image of God and called to prolong the work of creation."[15]

On the one hand, Catholic doctrine honors the person who is diligent in his work and significantly adds to the continuation of creation—economic development. Yet, Catholic doctrine warns of the sin of gluttony—work in pursuit of a disproportionate share of worldly goods. The person who acquires significant wealth through discovery of a medicine that cures a dreaded disease could be viewed as honorable by some and sinful by others. It seems that Catholic doctrine does not consider the accumulation of wealth as a sin, per se,

---

13. Michael Novak, *The Catholic Ethic and the Spirit of Capitalism* (New York: Free Press, 1993), 25.

14. Kreeft, *Catholic Christianity*, 198–99. The seven deadly sins are: pride, ava-rice, envy, wrath, sloth, lust, and gluttony.

15. Ibid., 264.

but the process by which wealth is accumulated is subject to question (e.g., through honest means).

Two additional writings from the Roman Catholic tradition are particularly worthy of review. The first is the papal letter from Pope Leo XIII, who served as pope between 1846 and 1878. His *Rerum Novarum*, released in 1891, not only addresses the charging of interest on loans but it was released during a critical time in world history—the time of the Industrial Revolution. The setting for this papal letter is important.

The second writing, *Centesimus Annus*, was released by Pope John Paul II in 1991 in celebration of the hundredth anniversary of *Rerum Novarum*. This contribution has the advantage of the observations of more modern times—in particular the experiments with socialism in the form of Communism and in what Pope John Paul II calls the Social Assistance State.

Rerum Novarum (1891)

Pope Leo XIII published *Rerum Novarum* in 1891, a time in which the Industrial Revolution in England and the United States was well entrenched. Both countries were overwhelmingly Protestant Christian. The full benefits of the Industrial Revolution had not visited countries with predominantly Catholic populations. This contrast greatly puzzled Catholic leaders. Would the growing standards of living observed in the major Protestant countries of the world, largely bypassing the many Catholic-dominated countries of the world, be a divinely guided change?

Pope Pius IX (1846–1878), Pope Leo XIII's predecessor, had pushed the church into isolation with his hostility to the world. The Catholic Church was "in its death throes."[16] Catholic colleges and universities were taken over by the state. Libraries were disbanded.

Rerum Novarum marked a turn from isolating Catholic thought from the changes in the world brought about by the Industrial Revolution to a direct confrontation with a more modern world, with increasing standards of living, a greater dependence upon world trade, and a growing inequality in income.

---

16. Novak, *The Catholic Ethic and the Spirit of Capitalism*, 40.

The contrast between growing prosperity and extreme poverty across nations after the Industrial Revolution was unprecedented. To a great extent, the United States was founded by the immigrants of Europe who were those looking for a better life. Many came from the lower classes of Europe while the landed gentry remained in Europe. How could a new nation largely consisting of the lower classes of Europe develop a growing economy, raising the standards of living above that of Europe, which retained the elite and intellectuals? Could it be that the new nation attracted more gifted people? Could it be that the Protestant expression of Christianity is favored by God? Could it be the differences in the systems of government and economic organization? *Rerum Novarum* provided some answers to these critical questions of the day.

Pope Leo XIII in this 1891 doctrinal letter condemned socialism, which had taken hold throughout much of Europe. Throughout much of Europe, governments weakened individuals' rights to property, including the incomes they earned. According to Pope Leo XIII,

> The Socialists... in endeavoring to transfer the possessions of individuals to the community, strike at the interests of every wage earner, for they deprive him of the liberty of disposing of his wages, and thus of all hope and possibility of increasing his stock and of bettering his condition in life. What is of still greater importance, however, is that the remedy they propose is manifestly against justice. For every man has by nature the right to possess property as his own. This is one of the chief points of distinction between man and the animal creation.[17]

The pope focused upon the importance of individuals' work ethic and the devastation caused through income redistribution. "Would justice permit anyone to own and enjoy that upon which another has toiled? As effects follow the cause producing them, so it is just that the fruit of labor belongs precisely to those who have performed the labor."[18]

The letter attacks systems that damage the incentives of the entrepreneur who creates the engines of economic growth. "If incentives to ingenuity and skill in individual persons were to be abolished, the very fountains of wealth would necessarily dry up; and the equality conjured

---

17. Pope Leo XIII, *Rerum Novarum*, encyclical letter, May 1891, para. 5, 6.
18. Ibid., para. 10.

up by the socialist imagination would, in reality, be nothing but uniform wretchedness and meanness for one and all, without distinction."[19]

Pope Leo XIII clearly understood and welcomed the differences in individuals, including talents, skills, health, and capacity. Differences in individuals are a blessing to society—not a curse.

> There are truly very great and very many natural differences among men. Neither the talents, nor the skill, nor the health, or the capacities of all are the same, and unequal fortune follows of itself upon necessary inequality in respect to these endowments. And clearly this condition of things is adapted to benefit both individuals and the community; for to carry on its affairs community life requires varied aptitudes and diverse services, and to perform these diverse services men are impelled most by differences in individual property holdings.[20]

The inequality of income is welcomed because of the important incentives to work such opportunities bring.

I recall one of my favored economic professors, Prof. Alfred F. Chalk, telling of an evening in which he was seated next to the CEO of a Fortune 500 corporation. He asked him if the extremely generous salary package he receives is important to him. His response was that the package is not at all important, for he has access and full privilege to corporate jets and corporate-owned properties all over the world. All of his needs are met before spending any of his salary. Yet, the size of the package encourages hundreds of MBAs to work very hard to climb the corporate ladder. It is the quest for such salary packages and benefits that cause key employees to give their best in their employment.

Centesimus Annus (1991)

Pope John Paul II authored *Centesimus Annus* in celebration of the hundredth anniversary of the publication of *Rerum Novarum* (1891). This 1991 papal letter fostered more than four thousand conferences to reflect upon the 1891 text from Pope Leo VIII. According to Pope John Paul II, "Not only is it wrong from the ethical point of view to disregard

---

19. Ibid., para. 22.
20. Ibid., para. 26.

human nature, which is made for freedom, but in practice it is impossible to do so. Where society is so organized as to reduce arbitrarily or even suppress the sphere in which freedom is legitimately exercised, the result is that life of society becomes progressively disorganized and goes into decline."[21] This is consistent with the economic theory expressed in Hayek, Friedman, and Becker and the empirical findings presented in Dollar and Kraay.

The pope observed the rise of the "welfare state" as implemented in the United States and other developed countries. In *Rerum Novarum*, the pope turns to a Catholic principle—subsidiarity. This is the principle that organizations closest to the problem are best positioned to solve it. A neighborhood is best positioned to solve a local problem rather than the state or the federal government.

This Catholic doctrine was developed out of the Second Vatican Council. This Council's work extended over the years, from 1962 to 1965, under the direction of two popes—Pope John XXIII and Pope Paul VI. Bishop Karol Wojtyla, who became Pope John Paul II, was in attendance. Although the principle of subsidiarity does not directly seek less government regulation and freer markets, it does seek more local regulation that best matches the local conditions regulations seek to improve. Centralized regulation is discouraged under this principle.

Father Sirico, in his latest book, argues that local governmental efforts to address the conditions of the poor can effectively take into account the work of private charities in place, thereby modifying governmental programs so as not to complete or replace these private charities.[22] This is an extremely important Catholic principle—seemingly ignored by most, if not all, Protestant denominations.

As to the wars on poverty, Pope John Paul II writes:

> In recent years the range of [state] intervention has vastly expanded, to the point of creating a new type of State, the so-called "Welfare State." This has happened in some countries in order to respond better to many needs and demands by remedying forms of poverty and deprivation unworthy of the human person. However, excesses and abuses, especially in recent years, have provoked very harsh criticisms of the Welfare State dubbed the

---

21.   John Paul II, *Centesimus Annus*, encyclical letter, May 1, 1991, para. 25.

22.   Robert Sirico, *Defending the Free Market: The Moral Case for a Free Economy* (Grand Rapids, MI: Acton Institute, 2012), 126.

"Social Assistance State." Malfunctions and defects in the Social Assistance State are the result of an inadequate understanding of the tasks proper to the State. Here again the principle of subsidiarity must be respected: a community of a higher order should not interfere in the internal life of a community of a lower order, depriving the latter of its functions, but rather should support it in case of need and help to coordinate its activity with the activities of the rest of society, always with a view to the common good.[23]

Note that this was a papal letter prepared in 1991—twenty-five years ago as of this writing. The extent of the dominance of social programs in the United States and throughout Europe at that time was but a shadow of its dominance today—especially in the United States.

The Catholic principle of subsidiarity is an important contribution to religious thought. Problems must be addressed at the lowest order—not the highest order. A child with reading difficulties should first be attended to by family members—not through rules and regulations adopted by state or federal governments. A person's physical disabilities should be accommodated by a local community's own prescriptions rather than a set of federal regulations established for all communities. An individual's lack of motivation to learn skills and to earn a living should be addressed within the local community rather than confounded with the federal and state provision of unemployment compensation, public housing, and food stamps.

The important messages from Catholic doctrine for our purposes are these:

- The dignity of humanity comes from God.

- Humans are made in the image of God and are to continue the work of creation through their dominion over the earth.

- A person's labor can be a hardship, imposed by God because of sin.

- Salvation comes from both faith and good works. Both are necessary.

- The extremes of socialism and capitalism can be destructive.

---

23. John Paul II, *Centesimus Annus*, encyclical letter, May 1, 1991, para. 25.

- Economic profits are necessary for sufficient investments in business, which drives employment.

- The accumulation of wealth can reflect honorable labor or the sin of gluttony.

- Socialism, as adopted in human history, has been destructive to human societies.

- Humans were created for the enjoyment of freedom and the rights to property.

- God's creation requires individual freedom, and the inequality of income results from individual freedom and the rights to private property.

- Public wars on poverty have not been successful.

- Subsidiarity must be understood and respected.

Chapter 6

Methodists

Gain all you can, by common sense, by using in your business all the understanding which God has given you.
—John Wesley

T he United Methodist Church and its immediate predecessor denominations are selected to represent the Protestant denominations. For much of the history of the United States, Methodists represented one of the largest Protestant denominations—particularly in the early decades of the twentieth century.[1] Of course, The United Methodist Church has lost more than 25 percent of its membership since its formation in 1968, suffering decline as have all mainline and most evangelical denominations.

From its very beginnings, England was a European country that was occupied by the Romans and had adopted Catholicism as its state religion. King Henry VIII sought an annulment with his Queen Catherine in order to marry Anne Boleyn, which required approval from the pope. His request from the pope was denied, England severed its ties with the Catholic Church, and the Church of England was established as England's own expression of Christianity—in 1534. The Church of England is considered both Catholic and reformed.

---

1. According to Roger Finke and Rodney Start, *The Churching of America, 1776–2005* (New Brunswick, NJ: Rutgers University Press, 2005), Methodists were twice as prevalent in the population in 1940 as Southern Baptists. They were three times more prevalent than Presbyterians. Southern Baptists surpassed the Methodists in numbers after 1960.

John and Charles Wesley were ordained clergy of the Church of England and remained loyal to this Protestant denomination. However, they formed their Methodist Societies throughout England in the eighteenth century, beginning as small groups of members of the Church of England (but also including Quakers, Presbyterians, and others), studying scripture, praying, and seeking deeper faith. As the colonies in the New World expanded through emigration from Europe, the Methodist societies grew and expanded in the colonies. Members of these societies worshipped in the Anglican congregations where possible. The American Revolution caused many clergy leading these congregations to return to England, leaving members of these Methodist societies without clergy to serve the sacraments, perform weddings and baptisms, and to bury the dead.

John Wesley authorized the establishment of the Methodist Episcopal Church in the newly formed United States, sending newly ordained bishops from England with foundational documents for which a new denomination could be established. During the originating conference held in Baltimore in 1784, the first *Book of Discipline* was adopted. This *Book of Discipline* has been edited, expanded, and refined during subsequent General Conferences ever since that time. Thus, the official records of General Conferences of the predecessor denominations of The United Methodist Church and The United Methodist Church itself provide critical explanations of doctrine that consider the rich, the poor, and the income gap between them.

Bishop Scott Jones, in *United Methodist Doctrine: The Extreme Center*, examines Wesleyan teaching and identifies four sources from which doctrine is presented: *Book of Discipline, Book of Resolutions*, Wesley's sermons, and *The United Methodist Hymnal*.[2] This quest is somewhat limited in that there are only four sources, and there is little in each of them that directly considers the inequality of income. The relevant parts of the *Book of Discipline* are few. In fact, the only relevant part is the Social Principles, which reflect policies from a diverse group of representatives but are not considered as binding as the church's constitution and articles of religion. The *Book of Resolutions* is a set of papers

---

2. Scott J. Jones, *United Methodist Doctrine: The Extreme Center* (Nashville: Abington Press, 2002), 47.

changed every four years, and, by design, papers are to remain in the *Book of Resolution* for only eight years unless they are renewed by action of the General Conference. The collection of papers, nevertheless, is an evolving expression of doctrine and policy. *The United Methodist Hymnal* is approved by the General Conference and contains some material pertinent to this inquiry.

The Book of Discipline

The *Book of Discipline* has the longest history, dating back to the late eighteenth century. For our question about wealth and poverty, we can pick up its evolution in 1960, before the accelerated decline in mainline denominations in the United States and before the social revolution, including race relations, the antiwar peace movements, the rise of feminism, and the antiestablishment mentality. The 1968 *Book of Discipline of The United Methodist Church* includes the following:

> Economic Order—The Church advocates equal rights and justice for all men in all stations of life; the protection of the family; ... the elimination of poverty; the equitable distribution of the products of agriculture and of industry; the abolishment of unemployment; a living wage in every vocation and economic justice for all; ... The Church advocates single, just, honest, unselfish and spiritual living, and stands not for an aristocracy of wealth, power, and position, but for an aristocracy of character, culture, and service.[3]

In addition to the assurance of rights and justice for all, the *Book of Discipline* emphasizes the importance of family as part of the economic order.[4] Interestingly, this is a recognition that continues through more modern studies.[5]

Note the interest in an equitable distribution of produce—not equal but equitable. Equitable refers to fair, just, and impartial. It does not refer to equality in the distribution of produce.

---

3. *The Book of Discipline of The United Methodist Church 1968*, 61. Emphasis added.

4. See, for example, paragraphs 161(A), 163(H), and 166.

5. Recall in chapter 2 the discussion of the paper by Becker and Murphy (2007).

The *Book of Discipline* seeks the end to unemployment and the fostering of a living wage in every vocation. The quest for a living wage has two opposing views. The first is the view of the employer—seeking a wage that yields funds sufficient for the employee to purchase adequate housing, food, clothing, and health care. The second view, one commonly ignored, is the employee's perspective. The employee must acquire skills, invest effort, and attend to the requirements of a job. This means that the employee must be worth a living wage in the marketplace—an employee who accomplishes assigned tasks and duties in a manner that requires the employer to pay a living wage in order to discourage the employee in seeking higher wages elsewhere.

The last sentences from the 1968 *Book of Discipline* are worthy of special attention. The term *aristocracy* refers to the highest class in a society. The doctrine of the church thus does not support aristocracy due to the accumulation of wealth, power, and position. The combination of the three, in contrast to treatment of each term independently, makes it clear that the church is not in support of those who wield power as a consequence of position and wealth. Stories and movies frequently develop characters who wield such power. Recall the jealous banker, Mr. Henry F. Potter, in the 1946 movie *It's a Wonderful Life*, who attempts to destroy the competing savings and loan in Bedford Falls, headed by George Bailey, played by the actor James Stewart. While there may be few such persons around, most who have seen the movie have a clear picture of the character—perhaps rare in reality.

In contrast, the church supports the high positions of those with character, culture, and service. This would, indeed, be George Bailey—a man who captures the respect of the entire town of Bedford Falls, one who has character, culture, and extends service to all. In the final scene in the movie many friends of George Bailey voluntarily collect more than enough money to cover the $8,000 bank deficit brought to the attention of the bank examiner at the hands of Mr. Potter. It is a feel-good movie but demonstrates the contrast posed in the *Book of Discipline* between the two types of aristocracies.

In this 1968 version of the *Book of Discipline*, there is nothing that suggests that a gap between the rich and the poor should be eliminated or even reduced in size. It calls for fair dealing, well-paid labor that requires personal dedication and attention to duty, and people of high character, culture, and service. It does not support those who wield power unjustly afforded by position and wealth.

For those over the age of sixty-five, we well remember the 1960s— an era that stands out as a time of change that set America on a new path. Legislation and Supreme Court decisions forced integration of schools, cafés, hotels, colleges, and universities, as well as many other public places. The Vietnam War prompted public demonstrations as young students burned draft cards and moved to Canada to avoid the compulsory draft. The heightened enforcement of women's rights in places of employment led to hiring quotas in many industries. Many student demonstrations, occasionally held on college campuses with takeovers of administration buildings, rejected the establishment wherever it might be found. Too often the evening news programs showed footage of riots in the cities, leaving property destroyed and occasional deaths. This, indeed, was a time of change.

One of the more influential books of the time was John Kenneth Galbraith's *The New Industrial State*, published in 1967, which became a best-selling book. In this book, Galbraith touted the evils of large corporations, which was welcomed by antiestablishment dissenters. This book and its followers promoted the distrust of large corporations and their owners. It is a theory and opinion, but it seems that this anti-business rhetoric crept into our churches and made possible changes in Christian-supported policies that were perhaps not possible before. The Social Principles in the *1972 Book of Discipline* is an example: "We support measures that would reduce the concentration of wealth in the hands of a few. We further support efforts to revise tax structures and eliminate governmental support programs that now benefit the wealthy at the expense of other persons.[6] ... In order to provide basic needs such as food, clothing, shelter, education, health care, and other necessities, ways must be found to more equitably share the resources of the world....To begin to alleviate poverty, we support such policies as: adequate income maintenance, quality education, decent housing, job training, meaningful employment opportunities, adequate medical and hospital care, and humanization and radical revisions of welfare programs."[7]

---

6. *The Book of Discipline of The United Methodist Church 1972*, 91. Emphasis added.

7. Ibid., 92–93.

This 1972 version of the Social Principles in the *Book of Discipline* is a significant departure from the earlier versions. It clearly establishes a distaste for an unequal distribution of income or wealth. There is no metric offered that would tell us at what level of inequality is there placed too much in the hands of a few. Yet the rhetoric disparages owners and managers of large businesses, not because they are proven to be sinful, evil people, but because they are found in positions of influence, which comes with the responsibilities of their respective positions.

John Wesley's Sermons

Before getting into John Wesley's sermons, a brief introduction into his general rules adopted in the administration of his Methodist societies in England is useful. Recall that the purpose of the Methodist societies was to encourage members to grow in their knowledge of scripture and in their faith. They were to remain active members of the Church of England. However, one was a member of the Church of England by being a citizen of England. The qualifications for membership were low. In contrast, qualification for membership in the Methodist societies included strict adherence to the following General Rules:[8]

Do no harm by avoiding evil of every kind.

Do good of every possible sort, as far as possible.

Attend to the ordinances of God (i.e., stay in love with God).

The first of the General Rules is particularly important—do no harm. It is something we will turn to in the later chapters.

One of John Wesley's sermons is particularly relevant to our primary interest—"The Use of Money." He preached this sermon twenty-five times between 1748 and 1759. It contains some of the most quoted Wesley principles of all: gain all you can, save all you can, and give all you can.

---

8. *The Book of Discipline of The United Methodist Church 2012*, paragraph 104, 76–78.

Each human is to gain all he or she can. This follows the nature-of-man doctrine found in Judaism and Catholicism—the human is made in the image of God and is to work in furthering creation. Judaism celebrates diligence, preparation in education and training, hard work, and the benefits of higher earnings. Wesley seems to agree. Judaism insists that one must attain earnings honestly. Wesley is more specific.

- Do not gain at the expense of physical health (depriving of food, sleep, clean air, sitting too long in an uneasy posture).

- Do not gain at the expense of one's mind (dealing in sinful trade, defrauding tax collectors, cheating, lying, or anything that injures the soul).

- Do nothing that hurts your neighbor (do not do evil that good might come, destroy his business in order to advance your own, entice away his servants or workmen, sell him anything that would impair his health).

His general rule, do no harm, is more limiting in these cautions and restrictions than merely being honest in one's endeavors—although honesty is a requirement.

> These cautions and restrictions being observed, it is the bounden duty of all who are engaged in worldly business to observe that first and great rule of Christian wisdom with respect to money, "Gain all you can by honest industry: use all possible diligence in your calling. Lose no time. If you understand yourself and your relation in God and man, you know you have none to spare. If you understand your particular calling as you ought, you will have no time that hangs upon your hands. Every business will afford some employment sufficient for every day and every hour. That wherein *you* are placed, if you follow it in earnest, will leave you no leisure for silly, unprofitable diversions."[9]

This part of the sermon acknowledges that a person might be employed where one's assigned tasks are not so pleasant. "That wherein

---

9. John Wesley, "The Use of Money," *Sermons II (34–70)*, ed. Albert C. Outlier, vol. 2 of The Bicentennial Edition of the Works of John Wesley (Nashville: Abingdon Press, 1985), 272–73.

you are placed" does not seem to refer to one's chosen profession or trade. This seems to adopt the Catholic recognition that work can be punishing at times. Recall that in Catholicism, a person is called to persevere in labor in unity with Christ, who suffered on the cross.

Wesley continues:

> Gain *all* you can, by common sense, by using in your business all the understanding which God has given you. It is amazing to observe how few do this; how men run on the same dull track with their forefathers. But whatever they do who know not God, this is no rule for *you*. It is a shame for a Christian not to improve upon *them* in whatever he takes in hand. *You* should be continually learning from the experience you have to do better today than you did yesterday. And see that you practice whatever you learn, that you may make the best of all that is in your hands.[10]

Wesley acknowledges that some will not be so diligent in their work and will fail to gain all they can. This is acceptance of the fact that there will be inequality of income. Yet there is no disparagement in success but disparagement in failure. And it is not success that is a gift from God. It is not a prosperity theology in which God grants material wealth among those who are dedicated followers of Christ. Wesley is encouraging dedication to one's work, and the marketplace will grant the rewards. The marketplace will not reward those who are not so diligent.

Wesley then turns to saving—once attaining the higher earnings gains through diligence, one must save all one can through careful spending.

> Having gained all you can, by honest wisdom and unwearied diligence, the second rule of Christian prudence is, *Save all you can.* . . . Do not waste any part of so precious a talent merely in gratifying the desires of the flesh; in procuring the pleasures of sense of whatever kind; particularly in enlarging the pleasure of tasting . . . there is a regular, reputable kind of sensuality, an elegant epicurism, which does not immediately disorder the stomach, nor (sensibly, at least) impair the understanding. And yet . . . it cannot be maintained without considerable expense. Cut off all this expense.[11]

---

10. Ibid., 273.
11. Ibid., 273–74.

And

> Lay out nothing to gratify the pride of life, to gain the admiration or praise of men.... Men are expensive in diet, or apparel, or furniture, not barely to please their appetite, or to gratify their eye, their imagination, but their vanity too. "So long as thou dost well unto thyself, men will speak good of thee."... No doubt many will applaud thy elegance of taste, thy generosity and hospitality. But do not buy their applause so dear. Rather be content with the honour that cometh from God.[12]

Wesley cautioned against the practice of "conspicuous consumption" that would be the topic of Thorstein Veblen's 1899 treatise, "*The Theory of the Leisure Class: An Economic Study in the Evolution of Institutions.*" This seems to support the cautions found in the earlier versions of the *Book of Discipline*, "The Church... stands not for an aristocracy of wealth, power, and position."[13]

Wesley supports the notion that one should gain the respect of others through Christian example. This is consistent with the often-cited adage—"Preach the gospel at all times, and when necessary, use words."

Although John Wesley had no children, he cautions parents in over-indulging them in material luxuries.

> And why should you throw away money upon your children, any more than upon yourself, in delicate food, in gay or costly apparel, in superfluities of any kind?... They do not want any more; they have enough already; nature has made ample provision for them. Why should you be at farther expense to increase their temptations and snares, and to "pierce them through with more sorrows"?[14]

Wesley sought for all Christians the attainment of high earnings while meeting the stated conditions and restrictions, and limited spending of those earnings. In 1781, Wesley preached his sermon entitled "The Danger of Riches," based upon 1 Timothy 6:9-10:

---

12. Ibid., 274–75.

13. Note the consistency between Wesley's cautions against wearing expensive apparel and the same discouragement found in Catholic doctrine (the sin of gluttony).

14. John Wesley, "The Use of Money," 275.

But people who are trying to get rich fall into temptation. They are trapped by many stupid and harmful passions that plunge people into ruin and destruction. The love of money is the root of all kinds of evil. Some have wandered away from the faith and have impaled themselves with a lot of pain because they made money their goal.

In this sermon, Wesley cautions us in accumulating excess wealth because of the temptations wealth brings—ignoring the happiness within God and seeking happiness elsewhere. One has excess wealth if it exceeds in value: (1) that which is necessary to provide the necessities and conveniences of life for those within our household; (2) that which is necessary for those in business to ensure the continuation of that business; (3) that which is necessary for our children so that they will be supplied with the necessities and conveniences of life; and (4) that which is necessary to cover all debts so that, at the end, one owes no one. It is the excess over these amounts that is of concern to Wesley.

Wesley provides a prescription for the accumulation of wealth in this sermon. The prescription, containing the four conditions, leaves to the reader a broad set of guidelines—especially for those with businesses. Preserving financial reserves in a business to ensure its continuation in the face of recessions and downturns in one's industry can require considerable sums—more than that maintained in most businesses. Nevertheless, Wesley provides for a generous allowance for the accumulation of wealth but seeks the avoidance of conspicuous spending.

One is tempted to quantify the income or wealth accumulation that Wesley would find acceptable today. Item number 2 alone supports a considerable accumulation of wealth among business owners. Economic downturns, whether general or within a specific industry, place considerable economic pressures upon businesses, and they often lead to bankruptcies when sufficient financial reserves have not been previously accumulated. Businesses often fail when they have insufficient cash to pay employees their scheduled wages or salaries. Reserves sufficient to weather the downturns can be considerable. Many never accumulate sufficient reserves.

Once a person has such reserves, through the accumulation of wealth necessary to attend to one's financial obligations, he or she should give the remainder away as charity. "If when this is done there be an overplus left, then 'do good to them that are of the household of faith.'"[15]

Wesley discards the notion of the tithe as too limiting in the amounts to give to charity. "'Render unto God' not a tenth, not a third, not half, but 'all that is God's,' be it more or less, by employing all on yourself, your household, the household of faith, and all mankind, in such a manner that you may give a good account of your stewardship when ye can be no longer stewards."[16]

It seems obvious that if one is to fully attend to Wesley's prescribed financial obligations (self, household, business, and debts) and have the "overplus" to give over a tenth of one's income to charity, one must be very diligent and dedicated in earning income. One's motivation for obtaining productive employment or establishing successful business is to financially support charitable causes. It is not greed that is to motivate one to achieve higher incomes. It is to acquire higher incomes in order to give more away.

In Wesley's mind, each member of a Methodist society who follows the General Rules, prepares oneself in education and training, tempers one's personal spending, avoids wasting time, and is diligent and dedicated to one's employment or business, will ultimately supply significant funds to charitable causes. Collectively, members of the Methodist societies could provide substantial amounts to charitable causes.

Methodist Hymns

Methodist doctrine is also expressed in the hymns they sing. Several hymns in *The United Methodist Hymnal* address the issues of work. Consider the following lines:

Forth in Thy Name, O Lord (Charles Wesley, 1749)

The task thy wisdom hath assigned, O let me cheerfully fulfill;
in all my works thy presence find, and prove thy good and perfect will.

---

15. Ibid., 277.
16. Ibid., 279.

Thee may I set at my right hand, whose eyes mine in-most substance
see,
and labor on at thy command, and offer all my works to thee.[17]

This Charles Wesley hymn sets forth the notion that God, as our creator, has assigned our specific tasks. It is particularly meaningful in the context of human duty to continue the work of creation—noted in Judaism and Catholicism. It is consistent with the understanding that each individual is unique and thus each has his or her own assignment.

Christ, from Whom All Blessings Flow (Charles Wesley, 1740)

Move and actuate and guide,
diverse gifts to each divide,
placed according to thy will,
let us all our work fulfill.[18]

Another Charles Wesley hymn acknowledges that each individual has been given a unique set of skills and abilities as set forth by our creator.

All Who Love and Serve Your City (Erik Routley, 1966)

In your day of wealth and plenty,
wasted work and wasted play,
call to mind the word of Jesus,
"Work ye yet while it is day."[19]

Erik Routley, in a more modern hymn, captures the Wesleyan call to earn all you can. It calls humans to continue to work in spite of the accumulation of wealth and plenty.

---

17. Charles Wesley, "Forth in Thy Name, O Lord," *The United Methodist Hymnal* (Nashville: The United Methodist Publishing House, 1989), 438, verses 2–3.

18. Charles Wesley, "Christ, from Whom All Blessings Flow," *The United Methodist Hymnal* (Nashville: The United Methodist Publishing House, 1989), 550, verse 3.

19. Erik Routley, "All Who Love and Serve Your City," *The United Methodist Hymnal* (Nashville: The United Methodist Publishing House, 1989), 433, verse 3.

We'll Understand It Better By and By (Charles Albert Tindley, 1906)

> We are often destitute of the things that life demands,
> want of food and want of shelter, thirsty hills and barren lands,
> we are trusting in the Lord, and according to God's word,
> we will understand it better by and by.
> By and by, when the morning comes,
> when the saints of God are gathered home,
> we'll tell the story how we've over-come,
> for we'll understand it better by and by.[20]

Charles Albert Tindley reminds us of the certainty that we will not be without the poor. Those who might be rich today might yet be poor tomorrow. This is a message to the poor. It seems that they shall not become dependent upon others but should persevere.

Christ Is Alive (Brian Wren, 1968)

> In every insult, rift, and war,
> where color, scorn, or wealth divide,
> he suffers still, yet loves the more,
> and lives, though ever crucified.[21]

Brian Wren acknowledges that there will be an unequal distribution of income, just as there are differences in skin color, war and peace, and insult and disparagement. Yet Christ continues his love of all.

God, That Madest Earth and Heaven (Frederick Lucian Hosmer, 1912)

> When the constant sun returning unseals our eyes,
> may we, born anew like morning, to labor rise.

---

20. Charles Albert Tindley, "We'll understand It Better By and By," *The United Methodist Hymnal* (Nashville: The United Methodist Publishing House, 1989), 525, verse 2.

21. Brian Wren, "Christ Is Alive," *The United Methodist Hymnal* (Nashville, The United Methodist Publishing House, 1989), 318, verse 4.

Gird us for the task that calls us, let not ease and self en-thrall us, strong through thee what-e'er befall us, O God most wise![22]

Frederick Lucian Hosmer, author of the second verse, encourages a strong work ethic. As with John Wesley, Hosmer seems to counsel against wasting time.

These hymns are consistent with the doctrine that humans are called to continue God's creation through dedicated work, best chosen for the set of skills and abilities God has provided. An unequal distribution of income should not be troubling. The poor should persevere in their station of life and not expect and demand the assistance of the more fortunate.

Methodist doctrine, as recorded among the three sources, established the following:

- Policies that would reduce the concentration of wealth in the hands of the few are to be supported.

- Tax structures that benefit the wealthy at the expense of the poor should be revised.

- Public programs that establish sufficient income maintenance should be supported.

- In caring for the poor, do no harm.

- Gain all you can, in honest manner, within the restrictions that protect self and do not injure neighbor.

- Save all you can without excessive accumulations that gratify pride or in pursuit of the admirations from other persons.

- Give all you can, once attending to one's personal financial obligations.

- Do not consider the biblical tithe (one-tenth) as a limit to what one should give.

---

22. Frederick Lucian Hosmer, "God, That Madest Earth and Heaven," *The United Methodist Hymnal* (Nashville, The United Methodist Publishing House, 1989), 688, verse 2.

Chapter 7

Key Scriptures on Wealth

In fact, it's easier for a camel to squeeze through the eye of a needle than for a rich person to enter God's kingdom.

—Matthew 19:24

The previous chapters present key understandings among several highly respected economists, and Jewish, Catholic, and Protestant doctrine as presented in the broader religious literature, in sermons and in hymns. In my own experience, not many church leaders have taken this particular journey in forming attitudes toward the rich, the poor, and the inequality of income. Yet, the journey is not quite complete. Now it is time to review selected scripture from the Christian Bible—scripture that is commonly referred to when the rich are considered in Sunday school classes, schools of mission, religious conferences, and a host of secular settings.

In spite of a rather selected review of materials, the purpose here is not to convince the reader that this is the one and only way to understand scripture. Instead, it is to offer another way of considering scripture that many readers might not have encountered. For me, it helped bring consistency to often-quoted scripture that beforehand seemed conflicted and personally troubling.

We begin with the last of the Ten Commandments, which sets boundaries to one's own consideration of the rich. We are instructed not to violate any of the Ten Commandments. Within Judaism, the Ten Commandments are the highest order of religious instruction. To be righteous in the eyes of God, these ten instructions must not be broken.

The Tenth Commandment is of particular interest within our journey.

> Do not desire your neighbor's house. Do not desire and try to take your neighbor's wife, male or female servant, ox, donkey, or anything else that belongs to your neighbor.[1]

This text establishes a litmus test in evaluating attitudes toward the rich and inequality of income. If such attitudes are partly or wholly based upon envy, they should be discounted—even discarded. These evaluations are difficult to manage since it is far too easy to add the envy label into one's argument when it might not apply. Moreover, it is difficult to understand the true basis of an attitude when envy is at play. Nevertheless, envy is often the basis for the disparagement of the rich.

Conspicuous consumption often fuels envy. Recall that Wesley cautions one against conspicuous consumption in his sermon on the spending of money. The avoidance of conspicuous consumption among the rich is an endearing quality—a true quality of Christian character. It is often not what one can afford that attracts respect from others. It is the expression of Christian character that attracts respect.

Most seeking a deeper understanding of Christian doctrine turn to the New Testament as their primary authority. Recorded teachings of Jesus are often the center of one's inquiry. Jesus's own words regularly trump anyone else's commentaries. A brief review of Jesus's life before his ministry is useful.

Recall that Jesus grew up in a Jewish home. The scripture records his earthly parents' annual trip to Jerusalem to celebrate the Passover. At the age of twelve after being separated from Joseph and Mary for three days, he was found in the temple:

> After three days they found him in the temple. He was sitting among the teachers, listening to them and putting questions to them.[2]

---

1. Exod 20:17.
2. Luke 2:46.

His knowledge of Jewish law, both written and oral, must have been reasonably complete. During his ministry, he expressed the importance of Jewish law:

> "Don't even begin to think that I have come to do away with the Law and the Prophets. I haven't come to do away with them but to fulfill them. I say to you very seriously that as long as heaven and earth exist, neither the smallest letter nor even the smallest stroke of a pen will be erased from the Law until everything there becomes a reality."[3]

This can be understood to mean that Jesus respected Jewish law and urged his followers to obey these laws—both written and oral laws. Thus, in interpreting Jesus's own words, especially his parables, it is reasonable to place these words in the context of Jewish law.

Recall also that Jesus was a carpenter from Nazareth, in the vicinity of the rebuilding of Sepphoris. Many of its residents were considered to be rich in their time. It is reasonable to assume that Jesus was acquainted with members of the upper class. Some might have been owners of property where he was practicing his trade. He likely received payment for his work from the rich. The rich were not individuals distant from his everyday life. As a follower of Jewish law, Jesus would have held some degree of admiration of the rich—especially those whose earnings were obtained honestly and shared generously with the poor.

Many biblical scholars in considering Jesus's perspectives on many subjects turn to the parables. Yet, as Walter Russell Bowie contends, the recordings of Jesus's parables may not have been perfectly transcribed:

> The parables of Jesus which are most characteristic of his teaching are those in which the story element is so direct and simple that the interest of the hearer is caught immediately and swept along its swift and vivid stream. And this is true, even though we have, as we must remember, only a partial echo of Jesus' words. Nobody wrote down what he said when he was speaking. Many years later when the Gospels came to be compiled, nobody could recall all the sentences he had used; but the central current of his thought flows through as unmistakably as the fresh waters of the Amazon flood out where sailors can drink from them far at sea. There is a quality in the parables which time and distance cannot dilute or destroy.[4]

---

3. Matt 5:17-18.

4. Walter Russell Bowie, "The Teaching of Jesus, The Parables," *The Interpreter's Bible*, ed. George Arthur Buttrick, vol. 3 (Nashville: Abingdon, 1951).

There are some parables repeated two or three times in the Gospels with differences in presentations. As demonstrated below, it can be useful to review the differences. It can also be useful to remember the context of Jewish oral law in Jesus's parables and Paul's letters.

With this in mind, we turn to the most often quoted scripture in the Bible when one is searching for guidance in living among the rich.

The Eye of the Needle

The parable of the rich man that portrays the difficulty of passing a camel through the eye of a needle is repeated in the Synoptic Gospels three times—in Matthew, Mark, and Luke. Obviously, each of these gospel writers felt it important enough to ensure its inclusion in their works. In spite of the fact that no one transcribed Jesus's words, as Bowie notes, the three presentations of the parable are almost identical. Their differences, however, are notable.

We begin with the presentation of the parable as written in Luke 18:

A certain ruler asked Jesus, "Good Teacher, what must I do to obtain eternal life?"

Jesus replied, "Why do you call me good? No one is good except the one God. You know the commandments: Don't commit adultery. Don't murder. Don't steal. Don't give false testimony. Honor your father and mother."

Then the ruler said, "I've kept all of these things since I was a boy."

When Jesus heard this, he said, "There's one more thing. Sell everything you own and distribute the money to the poor. Then you will have treasure in heaven. And come, follow me." When he heard these words, the man became sad because he was extremely rich.

When Jesus saw this, he said, "It's very hard for the wealthy to enter God's kingdom! It's easier for a camel to squeeze through the eye of a needle than for a rich person to enter God's kingdom."

Those who heard this said, "Then who can be saved?"

Jesus replied, "What is impossible for humans is possible for God."

Peter said, "Look, we left everything we own and followed you."

Jesus said to them, "I assure you that anyone who has left house, husband, wife, brothers, sisters, parents, or children because of God's kingdom will receive many times more in this age and eternal life in the coming age."[5]

---

5. Luke 18:18-30.

The differences among the three presentations will be considered shortly. For now, we can review the most common interpretations of Matthew's presentation in the absence of the context of Jewish doctrine and Jesus's life as a carpenter.

For most readers, the parable is simple. A rich man wants Jesus to show him how he can attain eternal life, and Jesus tells his disciples that no one who is rich can enter God's kingdom. Only if the rich man gives away all of his money can he even begin to qualify for eternal life. He would also have to give up family, friends, and profession or trade and then join those who travel with Christ throughout Judea. The reader then learns that the rich man rejects the invitation. The reader typically assumes that he values possessions more than eternal life. At the end, the reader is reminded that salvation comes from God. Such is the common understanding.

In the absence of a more complete context, the reader views the rich man as one who follows Jewish law but cannot gain salvation because of his accumulation of wealth. Presumably, rich people fail to sufficiently care for the poor since they value their possessions far more than salvation. Perhaps the accumulation of wealth is itself a sin, and repentance requires the complete disposal of all property. For the rich, salvation requires the vow of poverty. We Christians might look upon the rich as sinners and the poor as those with a closer relationship with God. With this casual understanding of the parable, it is natural to harbor resentment toward the rich, even without envy in one's mind.

Let's now turn to the differences in the presentations of the parable. If one agrees with Bowie, the three Gospels represent separate, independent, and imperfect efforts to record Jesus's actual words. Perhaps the best way the reader can understand the parables is to consider all three as a whole without discounting any one of them—if that's possible.

The Quest for Completeness or Perfection

The first notable difference in the three presentations is the following sentence found in the Gospel of Matthew:

Jesus said, "If you want to be complete, go, sell what you own, and give the money to the poor. Then you will have treasure in heaven. And come follow me.'"[6]

The reader of Matthew is presented with the quest to become a completely competent and whole disciple, which is what Wesleyans call sanctification. If he wants to become a prepared and complete disciple, this particular rich man must sell all possessions, give the money to the poor, leave his family and friends, and travel with Jesus and his disciples throughout Judea. Throughout the entire Bible, perfection, if understood as sinlessness, is not a requirement for salvation. God's grace offers salvation to all sinners who change their hearts and lives and trust in the faithfulness of Jesus. The rich man here is offered a chance to take the next step toward a disciplined, whole, and completely satisfying life, but he chooses to walk away.

The Talmud, as a commentary on Jewish law, contains hundreds of prescriptions of just resolutions to parties of disputes, accidents, and willful wrongdoing. Jewish law presumes that one struggles with sin in the quest for more complete holiness. Sin is ever-present in human life, and permanent. Complete avoidance of all sin is impossible.

Perhaps one typical reading of the parable sets up an impossible demand, inviting the rich man to become sin-free. That would be similar to being offered the unaided ability to fly. The rich man knows that he can't be sinless, so he rejects the offer. However, in this parable, the rich man is offered a better, more holy and disciplined life on the condition that he sells all of his possessions. Perhaps he was willing to sell all of his possessions, but he rejected the invitation because he knew he could not handle the discipline and struggle of becoming a complete Christ-follower. Here Jesus does not propose a categorical condemnation of the rich. The story reminds us that following Jesus completely with our whole bodies, hearts, and minds is not a cheap grace, a grace that is not even earned through our best efforts to help the poor.

---

6. Matt 19:21.

The Gift of Love

The Gospel of Mark states: "Jesus looked at him carefully and loved him. He said, 'You are lacking one thing. Go, sell what you own, and give the money to the poor. Then you will have treasure in heaven. And come, follow me.' But the man was dismayed at this statement and went away saddened, because he had many possessions."[7]

The reader of Mark is reminded that Jesus loved the rich man—missing in the other two Gospels stories. According to Jewish law, the rich must earn their riches honestly. He is a man made in the image of God—one who is called to continue the work of creation. The rich must be generous in attending to the needs of the poor. The rich man in the parable noted that he had been obedient to the law. Jesus, who understood the full meaning of the rich man's statements, loved him. Could this love for the man also include some degree of admiration if his accumulation of wealth was through honesty and integrity? Perhaps the reader, too, is invited to hold admiration for the rich man.

Consider the difference between Jesus's love for the rich man and his treatment of the money changers in the temple. Jesus loved him even though he was not willing to sell all of his possessions. Any prejudicial disparagement of the rich is not being Christlike according to the Gospel of Mark.

Privileges and Responsibilities

Now we can turn to the similarities among the Gospels. Consider the following verses in Matthew, which are virtually identical in Mark and Luke:

> Then Peter replied, "Look, we've left everything and followed you. What will we have?"
>
> Jesus said to them, "I assure you who have followed me that, when everything is made new, when the Human One sits on his magnificent throne, you also will sit on twelve thrones overseeing the twelve tribes of Israel. And all who have left houses, brothers, sisters, father, mother, chil-

---

7. Mark 10:21.

dren, or farms because of my name will receive one hundred times more and will inherit eternal life. But many who are first will be last. And many who are last will be first."[8]

The rich have their privileges—then and now. The rich often live in the nicest neighborhoods, are members of the best social clubs, maintain seats on the front rows during popular concerts, occupy the first-class seats on airplanes, and are often given the best tables in restaurants. They often come first.

The parable reminds the rich that the privileges earned on earth do not transfer to eternity. This is not a condemnation. Elsewhere in the scriptures, eternal life rids us all of the needs for material things.[9] Competition for scarce resources will come to an end. Being first or last is of no further consequence. The parable sends a message to the poor that in eternal life their earthly struggles will be over.

The rich also have their responsibilities. With access to considerable resources, the rich person has the ability to do great works. Today, the rich fund hospitals, churches, scholarships, and a host of other worthy endeavors. In assessing all the good that humans can do, the rich have the resources to out-do the rest of us. Yet the responsibilities are not always without challenges and difficulties. As we will learn in a following chapter, doing good through the use of financial resources, without doing harm, is a considerable challenge. Even for the rich, the lifting of the competition for scarce resources is a true blessing.

The Assurance

Yet, the central message from the parable is that all mortals, including this rich man, are to receive salvation only from God, and that even the grandest deeds are not sufficient to earn salvation.

> "It's very hard for the wealthy to enter God's kingdom! It's easier for a camel to squeeze through the eye of a needle than for a rich person to enter God's kingdom."

8. Matt 19:27-30.
9. 1 Tim 6:7.

Those who heard this said, "Then who can be saved?"
Jesus replied, "What is impossible for humans is possible for God."[10]

There is evidence from the scriptures and history that, at least during the time of Jesus's ministry, those who attended Temple worship included the rich, such as the scribes, the Pharisees, and the Sadducees.[11] In Acts 2:3 the poor, lame man begging for money was placed near the Temple gate, presumably because many of the rich would pass by. Perhaps there was the accepted notion that the rich were favored by God (if wealth were acquired with honesty and integrity). The poor did not fit the image of one who worked hard in the continuation of God's creation. If that be the case, the parable of the rich man would be Jesus's message that those who are rich are not favored over the poor, simply because they are rich. Perhaps this explains why Jesus spent time and attention with the poor as a demonstration that they are not discounted.

The rich man is not condemned in the parable with a prohibition from eternal life. Jesus claims that salvation comes from God and cannot be earned from the greatest works afforded only through significant expenditures of financial resources or simply achieving an admired position in society.

Perhaps this is not a parable in which Christians are taught that the rich are sinful because they are rich. Perhaps this is not a parable in which salvation comes only to those who make a vow of poverty. Yet, the parable declares that it is difficult for the rich to enter the kingdom of heaven. Since Jesus was a well-educated Jew, it is possible that the difficulty explained in this parable lies in their unique difficulties of following Jewish law as well as Jesus's teachings.

---

10. Luke 18:24-27.

11. Josephus "charazterizes the Sadducees as rich and aristocratic" (*The New Interpreter's Dictionary of the Bible*, vol. 5 [Nashville: Abingdon Press, 2009], 32.). Mark 12:30-40 "describes scribes as those who walk around in long robes expecting to be greeted in the marketplaces and given good seats in synagogues and banquets" (*New Interpreter's Dictionary of the Bible*, vol. 5, 138.). "The portrayal that is implicit in the Gospel accounts agrees with Josephus with regard to the assumption that the Pharisees were the most prominent and influential group in Palestinian Jewish life" (*The New Interpreter's Dictionary of the Bible*, vol. 4 [Nashville: Abingdon Press, 2009], 488.).

Jesus reminds us that even the rich man is loved by God. Perhaps Jesus was teaching the richness of life, not in the accumulations of possessions but in the ministry to others. This principle was part of Wesley's sermon on money—save all you can but limit your accumulated wealth to meet the four uses of money—ear-marking the rest to be given away to others.

The Love of Money and Dishonesty

The scriptures condemn the love of money as one's primary motivation. This is the condemnation of greed. The love of money, as expressed in the scriptures, relates to the Catholic listing of greed or avarice as a "capital vice."

Condemnation of the love of money is presented in the scriptures at least four times.

> The love of money is the root of all kinds of evil. Some have wandered away from the faith and have impaled themselves with a lot of pain because they made money their goal.[12]

> "No one can serve two masters. Either you will hate the one and love the other, or you will be loyal to the one and have contempt for the other. You cannot serve God and wealth."[13]

The letter addressed to Timothy and the writer of Matthew's Gospel are understood as advice to Gentiles who were perhaps uneducated in Jewish law. Perhaps "serving money" and the "love of money" are both considerations of greed or the quest for money at the expense of honesty, integrity, and generosity.

Luke's Gospel creates this link between "serving money" and dishonesty.

> "Whoever is faithful with little is also faithful with much, and the one who is dishonest with little is also dishonest with much. If you haven't been faithful with worldly wealth, who will trust you with true riches? If you

12.   1 Tim 6:10.
13.   Matt 6:24.

haven't been faithful with someone else's property, who will give you your own? No household servant can serve two masters. Either you will hate the one and love the other, or you will be loyal to the one and have contempt for the other. You cannot serve God and wealth."[14]

Taken as a whole set, the love of money entails dishonest conduct in acquiring wealth. Clearly, there were many among the rich who were honest and trustworthy. These passages do not condemn the rich as a universal condition. Instead, they follow the Jewish law in insisting upon honesty in one's work.

The letter of James presents one of the more impassioned condemnations of dishonesty in accumulating wealth:

> Pay attention, you wealthy people! Weep and moan over the miseries coming upon you. Your riches have rotted. Moths have destroyed your clothes. Your gold and silver have rusted, and their rust will be evidence against you. It will eat your flesh like fire. Consider the treasure you have hoarded in the last days. Listen! Hear the cries of the wages of your field hands. These are the wages you stole from those who harvested your fields. The cries of the harvesters have reached the ears of the Lord of heavenly forces.[15]

This is a strong condemnation of dishonesty, carried into Christian teachings. The rich are condemned if the gains are acquired through dishonest means. The parallel with Jewish law should be obvious.

The importance of honesty in one's work is made clear in the letter to Timothy:

> This saying is reliable: if anyone has a goal to be a supervisor in the church, they want a good thing. So the church's supervisor must be without fault. They should be faithful to their spouse, sober, modest, and honest. They should show hospitality and be skilled at teaching. They shouldn't be addicted to alcohol or a bully. Instead, they should be gentle, peaceable, and not greedy. They should manage their own household well—they should see that their children are obedient with complete respect, because if they don't know how to manage their own household, how can they take care of God's church? They shouldn't be new believers so that they won't become proud and fall under the devil's spell. They should also have a good reputation

---

14.   Luke 16:10-13.
15.   James 5:1-4.

with those outside the church so that they won't be embarrassed and fall into the devil's trap.[16]

These scriptures leave no room for confusion. Honesty, integrity, and trust are hallmarks of Christian character.

The more common disparagements of the rich are likely based upon the presumption that most wealth is attained through dishonest conduct. This suspicion is understandable in view of the messages from movies and from financial news broadcasts about the collapse of economic systems. The disparagement is not often based upon relationships with those who are rich. Dishonest conduct exists, among some of the rich and some of the poor. But such conduct is not universal. The scriptures do not condemn the rich because they are rich. The scriptures condemn sinful conduct, which applies to all.

Financial Independence of Others

Recall that Jewish law discourages all to become financially dependent upon others. This law is to be taught to members of the family, and charity is to be distributed first to members of the household to ensure that they do not become financially dependent upon others. The Apostle Paul, a well-educated Jew, carries this theme in his second letter to the Thessalonians, who had lost hope for the present day and stopped working because they thought that Jesus would come back at any minute:

> Brothers and sisters, we command you in the name of our Lord Jesus Christ to stay away from every brother or sister who lives an undisciplined life that is not in line with the traditions that you received from us. You yourselves know how you need to imitate us because we were not undisciplined when we were with you. We didn't eat anyone's food without paying for it. Instead, we worked night and day with effort and hard work so that we would not impose on you. We did this to give you an example to imitate, not because we didn't have a right to insist on financial support. Even when we were with you we were giving you this command: "If anyone doesn't want to work, they shouldn't eat." We hear that some of you are living an undisciplined life. They aren't working, but they are meddling in other people's business. By the Lord

---

16.   1 Tim 3:1-7.

Jesus Christ, we command and encourage such people to work quietly and put their own food on the table. Brothers and sisters, don't get discouraged in doing what is right.[17]

This pronouncement from one of the last works included in the New Testament also comes from the Jewish understanding of one's calling to be in creation. This religious understanding of the duty to engage in work is evident, but it is not evident that Jewish law seeks an earthly punishment for failure to follow these teachings. Paul goes far toward punishment for those who fail to follow this Jewish requirement. As we will see later, this passage served as a principle in the establishment of relief in the colonies and early America.

Much Is Expected

In Luke's parable of the disobedient slave, many remember: *To whom much has been given, much is expected:*

Peter said, "Lord, are you telling this parable for us or for everyone?"

The Lord replied, "Who are the faithful and wise managers whom the master will put in charge of his household servants, to give them their food at the proper time? Happy are the servants whom the master finds fulfilling their responsibilities when he comes. I assure you that the master will put them in charge of all his possessions.

"But suppose that these servants should say to themselves, My master is taking his time about coming. And suppose they began to beat the servants, both men and women, and to eat, drink, and get drunk. The master of those servants would come on a day when they weren't expecting him, at a time they couldn't predict. The master will cut them into pieces and assign them a place with the unfaithful. That servant who knew his master's will but didn't prepare for it or act on it will be beaten severely. The one who didn't know the master's will but who did things deserving punishment will be beaten only a little. Much will be demanded from everyone who has been given much, and from the one who has been entrusted with much, even more will be asked."[18]

---

17. 2 Thess 3:6-13.
18. Luke 12:41-48.

This parable speaks of the possession of knowledge about when Christ returns—not the possession of property or wealth. The reader commonly focuses only upon the last sentence and applies this to the possession of property. It sets up an expectation that the wealthy must demonstrate considerable acts of charity. Yet the context is knowledge of the end times—not riches.

It is interesting that this common interpretation is most consistent with Jewish law. The wealthy are to share this wealth with others. Yet Jewish law gives the wealthy the right and privilege of choosing how to share, and family comes first. This parable does not seem to give the reader the authority to disparage the rich man because he does not give to charitable causes targeting the poor.

The next parable comes from Matthew's Gospel. It is the parable from which we often say, "What you have done to the least of these, you have also done unto me."

> "Then the king will say to those on his right, 'Come, you who will receive good things from my Father. Inherit the kingdom that was prepared for you before the world began. I was hungry and you gave me food to eat. I was thirsty and you gave me a drink. I was a stranger and you welcomed me. I was naked and you gave me clothes to wear. I was sick and you took care of me. I was in prison and you visited me.'
>
> "Then those who are righteous will reply to him, 'Lord, when did we see you hungry and feed you, or thirsty and give you a drink? When did we see you as a stranger and welcome you, or naked and give you clothes to wear? When did we see you sick or in prison and visit you?'
>
> "Then the king will reply to them, 'I assure you that when you have done it for one of the least of these brothers and sisters of mine, you have done it for me.'"[19]

This parable makes it quite clear that Christians are called to help the needy. It served as the foundation for one of the most loved Christmas poems, "The Christmas Guest." This scripture serves to motivate Christians and non-Christians to provide food, clothing, and drink to those in need. It calls for us to care for the ill and to visit those imprisoned. It demands that we get involved with the sick and the impris-

---

19.   Matt 25:34-40.

oned—involved more than merely providing financial support. No part of this parable singles out the rich.

Overview

The biblical support for disparagement of the rich comes most often from the parable of the rich man and the use of the image of a camel passing through the eye of a needle. A careful examination of this parable, in the context of Jewish law, seems to say that the rich are loved but face difficult responsibilities that come from wealth. Jesus offers compassion to the rich man and reminds the reader that the rich cannot attain eternal life through good works. Salvation comes only through the unmerited grace of God as obtained through the faithfulness of Jesus on the cross. A sense of disparagement toward the rich through this parable is misplaced.

Consistent with Jewish law, the rich face the temptation of placing the attainment of wealth as a priority of life. Admiration of the rich comes only if the attainment is reached honestly and with integrity.[20] With the accumulation of wealth comes the responsibility of generosity, and this responsibility must not be taken lightly. Failing to render aid to those in need is equivalent to withholding aid from Christ himself.

Also consistent with Jewish law, Christians are to financially prosper to the extent of remaining financially independent of others. This incorporates a strong work ethic. For those who refuse to work, food or subsistence should not be provided. Although this teaching might seem harsh, perhaps a form of "tough love," it belongs within Christian doctrine.

The major points from the New Testament parables and letters are these:

---

20. From Judaism, one can admire the rich man or woman who follows the law and dedicates himself or herself to the continuing work of God's creation. A singer might be admired because of a great voice. The singer might be wealthy through the honest distribution and sale of his or her music. Admiration, in such an instance, is unlikely to be accompanied with envy.

- A careful reading of the parable of the rich man fails to offer any support for a general disparagement of the rich.

- This parable, when placing Jesus in the context of Jewish law, extends a sense of compassion for the rich.

- The tenth Commandment, avoiding envy, often fosters disparagement of the rich.

- The parable reminds us that salvation cannot be earned through good works but is offered as a gift only from God.

- We all face the temptation of placing the attainment of wealth as life's priority.

- Consistent with Jewish law, the attainment of wealth must be done so with honesty and integrity.

- Consistent with Jewish law, Christians must seek to remain financially independent of others.

The Poor and Charity in the United States

"Give us strength to aid the helpless. Rid our hearts of selfishness. Teach us mercy, humility, and charity. Make us thoughtful of the sick, the unfortunate, and the needy. Make our humble lives a reflection of thy goodness."

—Excerpt from a prayer at suppertime in the 1938 movie
Of Human Hearts

The historical development of charity in the United States is important for several reasons. First, the United States was founded in large part by those seeking religious freedom. Several of the original thirteen colonies were settled by Protestant groups, establishing somewhat restrictive state laws that favored a particular Christian perspective. Second, it was a new nation without existing laws and regulations that favored selected industries, trades, or professions over others. As will be noted below, there was no apparent class order that would inhibit the mobility among income levels. Most had the economic and social freedom to join the wealthy, and the wealthy could quickly slip into poverty.[1] Third, there was a strong sense of compassion for the disadvantaged, and society was unencumbered with strong customs and institutions that limited the freedom to experiment and

---

1. Of course, those enslaved in early America did not have the freedom necessary to improve their stations in life.

establish new methods of helping the poor and disadvantaged. It is useful to examine the solutions that were implemented in early America and observe how those solutions were replaced with our current provisions as entitlements.

Early America was a country of immigrants, many of whom were escaping difficult economic conditions in Europe. Many immigrants arrived in America with little or nothing. The inflow of immigrants from Europe was not steady but changed with the conditions in Europe. For instance, the Great Famine in Ireland from 1845 to 1852 led to substantial emigration to America. By 1850, the Irish represented a quarter of the populations in Boston, New York, Philadelphia, and Baltimore. As noted below, the inflow of immigrants into America's major cities overwhelmed the work of private charities and fostered much of the development of government-sponsored relief programs for the poor.

Marvin Olasky reports in his book *The Tragedy of American Compassion* that charity in early America was largely driven by religious convictions: "the belief that God's law overarched every aspect of life suggested that the most important need of the poor who were unfaithful was to learn about God and God's expectations for man. Spiritual as well as material help was a matter of obligation rather than request."[2]

Religious beliefs were paramount, and the concern for the poor included all the needs of the poor—not just their material needs.[3] A broader concern for the whole person was inspired by scripture calling sinners to follow Christ and for Christians to find and keep employment. Paul's second letter to the Thessalonians, as noted in the previous chapter, may have been a source of inspiration:[4]

---

2. Olasky, *The Tragedy of American Compassion* (Wheaton, IL: Crossway Books, 1992), 8–9.

3. Olasky noted that the Methodists adopted John Wesley's quote "Put yourself in the place of every poor man and deal with him as you would [have] God deal with you." Gertrude Himmelfarb in *The Idea of Poverty: England in the Early Industrial Age* (New York: Knopf, 1984), 32, quoted in Olasky, *Tragedy of American Compassion*, 8.

4. Olasky reports the dependence of this scripture by the Society for Encouraging Industry and Employing the Poor in 1752. See Olasky, *Tragedy of American Compassion*, 10.

> You yourselves know how you need to imitate us because we were not un-
> disciplined when we were with you. We didn't eat anyone's food without
> paying for it. Instead, we worked night and day with effort and hard work
> so that we would not impose on you. We did this to give you an example
> to imitate, not because we didn't have a right to insist on financial support.[5]

Emphasis on the whole person was a common theme. In 1698,
Cotton Mather, a pastor, noted: "you may not *abuse* your charity by
misapplying it.... Let us try to do good with as much application of
mind as wicked men employ in doing evil."[6]

One of the major points here is the concern for a fragile work ethic.
Judaism, Catholicism, and Protestantism each incorporate into their respective doctrine the importance of the work ethic. Wesley, in particular,
cautions against doing harm. Paul's second letter to the Thessalonians
is abundantly clear. In whatever the method and style of charity toward
the poor, the protection of the work ethic is crucial.

Charity expressed in the nineteenth century by religious and civic
organizations demonstrate strong allegiance to this Christian doctrine,

> to give to one who begs... or in any way to supersede the necessity of indus-
> try, or forethought, and of proper self-restraint and self-denial, is at once to
> do wrong, and to encourage the receivers of our alms to wrong doing... a
> clear perception, and a faithful avoidance of the evils, of an injudicious
> bestowment of alms, is essential to Christian alms-giving.... We are not un-
> necessarily to do evil by the means by which we may, and should do good.[7]

Again, the preservation of the work ethic was understood, and the
provisions of charity in a manner that damages the work ethic was to
do evil.

It was challenging to provide charity without injuring the work
ethic. At least two principles were adopted: the provision of charity
was coupled with the requirement of work and those receiving charity were not to find comfort in that lifestyle. The first principle led to

---

5. 2 Thess 3:7–9.

6. Robert H. Bremmer, *American Philanthropy* (Chicago: University of Chicago
Press, 1960), 14, quoted in Olasky, *Tragedy of American Compassion*, 9.

7. Association of Delegates from the Benevolent Societies of Boston, *First Annual Report* (Boston: I. R. Butts, 1835), 7–44, quoted in Olasky, *Tragedy of American
Compassion*, 19.

the establishment of workhouses in which the men often would be required to chop wood and the women would sew to qualify for food and lodging. The charitable societies experienced those seeking food and lodging where the requirements of work were either minimal or absent. There were those who shopped for the preferred relief outlet. Charitable societies would often coordinate their policies in order to discourage relief shopping.

The Benevolent Societies of Ohio, for example, adopted the following rule: "If any poor person shall refuse to be lodged, kept, maintained, and employed in such house or houses, he or she shall not be entitled to receive relief from the overseers during such refusal."[8]

These rules, of course, did not apply to the disabled or those incapable of work. Olasky finds that there were diligent efforts to maintain strict rules among the benevolent societies that protect the work ethic. Any single charitable organization could hinder the success of others. "Those who gave material aid without requiring even the smallest return were considered as much a threat to true compassion as those who turned their backs on neighbors and brothers."[9]

There was a real sense that bad charity would drive out the good. History proved that this intuition was a correct one.

Olasky reports of experience in New Haven, Connecticut, where S. O. Preston found that "fewer than one out of a hundred refused to work in the woodyard or sewing room, perhaps because 'there is no other institution in this city where lodging can be secured except by cash payments for the same.'"[10] In contrast, "After several years of easygoing charity in Oregon, N. R. Walpole of Portland 'found among the unemployed a reluctance to work, and regarded compulsory work as the only solution of the problem.'"[11]

---

8.   Salmon P. Chase, ed., *The Statutes of Ohio and the Northwestern Territory*, vol. 1 (Cincinnati: Corey and Fairbanks, 1833), 176, quoted in Olasky, *Tragedy of American Compassion*, 12.

9.   Olasky, *Tragedy of American Compassion*, 21.

10.   S. O. Preston, "Night Work in the Woodyard," *The Charities Review II*, November 1892, 42, quoted in Olasky, *Tragedy of American Compassion*, 110.

11.   John Glenn, "Cooperation Against Beggary," *The Charities Review I*, December 1891, 46, quoted in Olasky, *Tragedy of American Compassion*, 110.

There developed a true sense of charity causing harm and making things worse rather than better. Those engaged in the delivery of charity celebrated the successes but understood through experience that charity could create a "tribe of 'frauds' and 'professional beggars.' Those dispensing charity in any form were to take a hard line lest your efforts will merely increase the numbers seeking charity and promote the very conduct that charities were seeking to eliminate." This seems consistent with Wesley's General Rules—do no harm. The provision of charity that would injure or destroy the work ethic is worse than having in place no charity at all.

Strong principles were established among many charitable organizations and churches. First, the development and protection of the work ethic was an important step in promoting and maintaining good character.[12] Second, providing no relief to the able-bodied was to rely upon discomfort and even hunger to motivate them to find and maintain employment.[13] Man was not to rely upon others for the provision of his necessities and comfort. This Christian life was one in which man was to assume his own responsibility for such things.

There was to be a sense of discomfort for those living off the wages of others. Jacob Riis was a successful journalist, photographer, and writer, having spent years of living in urban poverty. He was a student of the causes of poverty and its maintenance. He was an important friend of Theodore Roosevelt, who was reportedly influenced by Riis's understanding of the causes of poverty. According to Olasky, "Although he [Riis] did not oppose all governmental welfare, he did not want payment to be a right, since he wanted the subsidized to feel guilty."[14] To Riis, "It is money scattered without judgment—not poverty—that makes the pauper."[15] Further, "The stigma which fortunately attaches to *public* relief...

---

12. Olasky, *Tragedy of American Compassion*, 77. Josephine Shaw Lowell, of New York's Charity Organization Society, concludes "no man can receive as a gift what he should earn by his own labor without a moral deterioration."

13. Olasky, *Tragedy of American Compassion*, 105. Jacob Riis writes: "the way to fight 'real suffering in the homes of the poor' was to hang tough on 'enforcing Paul's plan of starving the drones into the paths of self-support: no work, nothing to eat.'"

14. Olasky, *Tragedy of American Compassion*, 116.

15. Otto L. Bettman, *The Good Old Days—They Were Terrible* (New York: Random House, 1974), 12, 96, 115, 129, quoted in Olasky, *Tragedy of American Compassion*, 116.

prevents creation of an 'incentive to parents to place their children upon the public for support.' "[16]

Having lived as a pauper, Riis encountered many able-bodied individuals satisfied to remain poor so as to avoid work. To Riis, "an impoverished person was perched precariously halfway up the ladder, capable of being helped toward independence or pushed (often by those with good intentions) into the pit of pauperism."[17]

Again, the fragile work ethic was to be protected. The condition of dependence was to be temporary and discouraged. The charitable societies understood the challenges they faced. They acknowledged the importance of one-on-one ministries to the poor, and they "agreed that relief should be given only after a 'personal examination of each case,' and 'not in money, but in the necessities required in the case.' "[18]

Interactions with the poor were common and encouraged in New Haven prior to the Civil War:

> The importance of personal involvement of rich and poor was still stressed year after year. . . . Cities were growing throughout the antebellum period but were still generally compact, with rich and poor living near each other. Those who were better-off regularly saw different neighborhoods as they walked to work, and they worshiped among neighbors from various social and economic backgrounds.[19]

Personal involvement was the primary method by which the amount and type of relief could be customized for the individual in need. The notion of equal treatment was largely rejected. Olasky reports: "Social thought of this period did not insist on equal treatment for all who were in trouble. The goal, rather, was to serve individuals who had unavoidable problems."[20]

---

16. Jacob Riis, *The Children of the Poor* (New York: Scribner's, 1892), 277–78, quoted in Olasky, *Tragedy of American Compassion*, 116–17.

17. Olasky, *Tragedy of American Compassion*, 116.

18. Association of Delegates from the Benevolent Societies of Boston, *First Annual Report* (Boston: I. R. Butts, 1835), 7–44, quoted in Olasky, *Tragedy of American Compassion*, 19.

19. Olasky, *Tragedy of American Compassion*, 17.

20. Ibid., 16.

Small-scale personal involvement was preferred to categorizing groups of individuals with similar needs and treating them equally. Every individual in need was unique and was worthy of relief customized for his or her individual benefit. Of course, the private charities were capable of avoiding this categorization.

The reported successes of private charity were remarkable in larger cities, such as New York. Olasky reports: "one charity group over eight years raised '4,500 families out of the rut of pauperism into proud, if modest, independence, without alms'...another 'handful of noble women...accomplished what no machinery of government availed to do. Sixty thousand children have been rescued by them from the streets.'"[21] An important record of a traveling visitor in Ohio during the 1830s illustrates the common absence of beggars on the streets. "The Traveller's feelings are not harrowed at every turn by the sight of some squalid, ragged, wretched object in human shape. Indeed, during the whole two years of my residence in America, I saw but one beggar.'...One 'disabled Scotchman'...received free 'board amongst the farmers, sometimes at one house, and sometimes another.'"[22] These examples strongly suggest that the principles adopted by many private charities in early America led to effective relief programs—providing relief to those in need while protecting the work ethic.

Olasky's review of this early American history yields "marks of compassion." His seven seals of good philanthropic practice are listed as follows:[23]

- **Affiliation**: restoring family ties, re-involvement with religious groups

- **Bonding**: attachments with volunteers

- **Categorization**: unequal treatment and care

---

21. Jacob Riis, *How the Other Half Lives* (New York: Dover, 1971 [1890]), 151, 199, quoted in Olasky, *Tragedy of American Compassion*, 101.

22. D. Griffiths Jr., *Two Years' Residence in the New Settlements of Ohio, North America: with Direction to Emigrants* (London: Westley and Davis, 1835), 37, 76–77, quoted in Olasky, *Tragedy of American Compassion*, 22.

23. Olasky, *Tragedy of American Compassion*, 99–115.

- **Discernment**: a new attitude toward the poor

- **Employment**: among able bodied, long term

- **Freedom**: employment without bribes

- **God**: close relationship with one's creator

As Olasky notes, it is impossible from the available evidence to establish reliable statistics that measure the success of their efforts. However, the records are filled with examples of charity workers being personally involved in the lives of those being assisted. Large numbers of individuals in poverty returned to productive employment. Charities recognized that mere distribution of money to the poor created distance between those providing charity and those receiving charity. More importantly, such distributions were often, perhaps usually, counterproductive.

This early American charity was apparently well-grounded in religious doctrine. Judaism calls people into productive work, and idleness is not to be tolerated. Olasky finds that the Apostle Paul's second letter to the Thessalonians is recorded in multiple early American documents. Many charities emphasized the establishment of personal relationships between those providing relief and those receiving relief. Charities in many places commonly adopted standards so that work requirements for the able bodied could be successfully enforced. The notion that bad charity drives out good charity appears to have been an accepted principle.

The plight of private charities, including the churches, synagogues, and religious charities, was not a promising one by the end of the 1800s. There was a growing interest in expanding the number of individuals being helped by charity. Many were becoming impatient with the slow process of one-on-one service. Additionally, the United States experienced in the early 1900s an unprecedented inflow of immigrants, including large Jewish populations, from Eastern Europe who were fleeing religious and social persecution. Table 1 illustrates this substantial shift in the number of immigrants over the period.

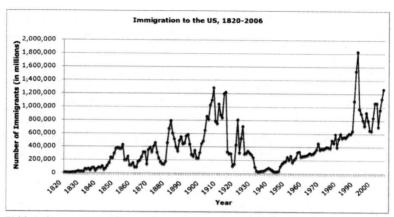

Table 1 (Source: U. S. Department of Homeland Security, *Yearbook of Immigration Statistics, 2006*, Washington, DC, U. S. Department of Homeland Security, Office of Immigration Statistics, 2007.)

The inflow of immigrants into the larger cities outpaced the growth of employment, causing ever-increasing numbers falling into poverty. This was particularly evident between 1900 and 1920. It was during this time that the cry for large-scale relief reportedly dominated the cries for one-on-one charities that had been the standards for so long.

The winds of change were becoming stronger. Beginning in the 1900s with the rapid increase in the number of immigrants into the United States, there seemed to have been a shift in priorities in dealing with the poor. There was a growing belief that private charities could not handle the scale of poverty developing in the cities where the new immigrants were concentrating. It was believed that governments should begin taking some levels of responsibility due to its capacities to supply relief fueled by tax revenues. Private charities were dependent upon voluntary contributions that could not compete with the funds governments could assemble through taxation.

More importantly, there was a rejection of the religious doctrine that had guided the provision of charities to the poor. Recall that Jewish law cautions one not to encourage financial dependence upon others. The Apostle Paul instructed the Christians awaiting the end times in Thessalonica to earn what is required for living expenses and not become dependent upon others as an example of Christian living. "If anyone doesn't want to work they shouldn't eat."[24] This principle was the religious foundation for the establishment of the workhouses. Moreover, there was an insistence to address the spiritual needs of the poor. Although less capable of dealing with thousands of impoverished families at a time, the forms of charity were to be tailored to the specific needs of the individuals. This required more personal involvement in the lives of those being assisted.

Christian doctrines were to be dismissed in favor of new emphases. The changes became apparent at the turn of the century. Editors of the *Christian Century* in 1900, quoted by Olasky, wrote: "A great breaking up, a spring thaw, is going on in the religious world.... Our 'old faiths' must be viewed in 'new lights.'...We cannot pin our faith to Calvin or Luther, Wesley or Campbell. Much less can we pin our faith to old forms. The living, loving Christ alone is sufficient."[25]

By 1922, many had turned to government as the proper administrator and provider of relief. Frank Dekker Watson, a sociology professor at Haverford College, argued that private charities might be used as an excuse for government to "evade the responsibility." Private charities were beginning to be viewed as evidence of government failures. Universally, all charitable needs should be provided through government programs.[26]

According to Olasky, "Studies in human evolution and social processes were said to provide understanding that required reinterpretation of the Bible, since God was now most visible 'in the great common places of life, in nature, in the long evolutionary process.'[27] Biblical statements could not be taken literally."[28]

The new emphasis seems to have discarded the relevant features of Jewish law and Paul's letters, in favor of a shallow application of the

---

24. 2 Thess 3:10.

25. *Christian Century*, May 10, 1900, 5, quoted in Olasky, *Tragedy of American Compassion*, 136.

26. Frank Dekker Watson, *The Charity Organization Movement in the United States* (New York: Macmillan, 1922), 332, 398–99, 527, quoted in Olasky, *Tragedy of American Compassion*, 137–38.

27. *Christian Century*, September 2, 1909, quoted in Olasky, *Tragedy of American Compassion*, 136.

28. "Fundamentalism, Modernism and the Bible," *Christian Century*, April 3, 1924, 424–26, and editorials of March 27, 388–90, and April 17, 495–97, quoted in Olasky, *Tragedy of American Compassion*, 136.

statement by Jesus, "When you have done it for one of the least of these brothers and sisters of mine, you have done it for me." Relief programs need only to provide food, shelter, and clothing to those in need.

Remarkably, there was an understanding that the provision of food, shelter, and clothing would naturally lead to an improvement in morality among those being served: "Since... theological liberals assumed that individuals freed from material pressures would also be freed from the sinful tendencies assumedly growing out of those pressures, the focus increasingly was on material needs."[29] According to Hall Caine, author of *The Christian*, "People are better housed, and for that reason, among others, their morality has improved."[30]

Of course, there is little use in searching for any scientific studies that support the new theology that encourages the provision of food, clothing, and shelter without regard to one's work ethic or one's religious faith. Religious people were to blindly accept the more modern notions of human development, disregarding religious doctrine that had served to guide humankind for centuries.

The movement toward public programs in place of private charities was fueled by the editors and owners of newspapers, which was the dominant source of information in those days. Olasky reports that William Randolph Hearst, owner of the largest newspaper chain in the United States, promoted the concept of public provisions of relief on grand scales—even calling for guaranteed incomes for the poor.[31]

Journalists began emphasizing "inputs" rather than "outputs." The successful charitable efforts were those that could feed thousands without regard to how many found employment and were no longer dependent. Private charities could not compete with the scale of government programs in their distribution of financial support even though the private charities likely better controlled the number seeking support and in moving people off dependency. There are those that claim that you get more of whatever you measure. The shift to counting the number

29. Olasky, *Tragedy of American Compassion*, 138.

30. Hall Caine, "Mission of the Twentieth Century," *Chicago Tribune*, December 30, 1900, quoted in Olasky, *Tragedy of American Compassion*, 138.

31. US Congress, Senate, *Conference on Care of Dependent Children: Proceedings*, 60th Cong., 2d sess., 1909, S. Doc. 721, quoted in Olasky, *Tragedy of American Compassion*, 138–39.

of people receiving aid clearly promoted an increase in the number seeking aid.

In the early 1900s, the substantial growth in government provision of entitlements and its assumed responsibility for the poor began. Although incomplete, the following list of government programs is notable:

1909   Children's Bureau

1921   Sheppard-Tower Act (child welfare)

1932   Federal Emergency Relief Administration, WPA

1935   Social Security Act

1960s   War on Poverty, Great Society, Medicare, Medicaid

1997   Children's Health Insurance Program (CHIP)

2010   Affordable Care Act

Olasky reports that the federal government had rejected the assumption of new powers that would justify entry into the business of relief for the poor. A milestone in this long-established rejection occurred in 1854 when a proposal to require the federal government to provide funding for mental hospitals was rejected.

The beginning of these new federal powers traces back to a White House Conference on Care of Dependent Children in January 1909 under President Theodore Roosevelt. Olasky notes that the president admitted: "How the relief shall come, public, private, or by a mixture of both, in what way, you are competent to say and I am not."[32]

Although many states had already enacted legislation providing assistance to children without fathers in the home, the assumption of responsibilities by the federal government entailed months of debates. President Roosevelt cautioned the Congress to require the federal gov-

---

32. US Congress, Senate, *Conference on Care of Dependent Children: Proceedings*, 60th Congress, 2nd Session, 1909, Doc. 721, quoted in Olasky, *Tragedy of American Compassion*, 138.

ernment to allow the public to continually evaluate and perhaps restrict the operations of the children's bureau with "full knowledge of the facts."

The move toward federal involvement in the provision of relief to the poor was somewhat tentative in its beginning but was based upon a disregard of the principal religious doctrine that had shaped American compassion for over a century. The movement was fueled by rapid immigration into the major cities at rates for which industry could not keep pace with the inflow of workers through expanding productive and by an acceptance of new understandings of human development.

I recall a conversation in the early 1980s in my hometown with a director of a private, local food bank. Upon observing many individuals receiving free groceries, complaining of completing forms before returning to their expensive automobiles, the director confessed that this is the "price" of getting the food to those really deserving clients.

What the director perhaps missed was the dependency created among those taking advantage of the program. Our review of religious doctrine seems to contend that the harm caused among many individuals may be sufficient to discontinue many existing programs. This is what some writers refer to as the "warm glow." It is a focus upon the good feelings of the giver without regard to the total impact upon the receivers. To protect the magnitude of the warm glow, the administrator and supporters are unwilling to even investigate the level of dependence and harm caused with indiscriminant provision of groceries.

The modern emphasis upon the indiscriminant provision of material goods is a great departure from the more deliberate, personal care for the poor as demonstrated in early America. It seems that early practices were grounded in biblical scripture and targeted the physical needs of the poor but combined the concern for physical needs with the concern for one's work ethic and morals. Financial dependence upon others among the able bodied was viewed as a temporary condition to be addressed as if it were a curable disease.

The changes in methods by which care has been provided to the poor have been substantial. There are important lessons to be learned from this history:

- Many who came to America in the 1700s arrived with few possessions, facing the uncertainties of a new world.

101

- Some struggled with hardships and fell into poverty.

- Charitable societies formed to render aid to the poor.

- Societies adopted common principles and practices.

- These practices sought to provide relief without damaging the individual's work ethic and moral character.

- Building personal relationships with the poor was necessary to individualize relief so that one could quickly return to financial independence.

- In the interest of efficiencies and increased scale, the work of charitable societies was discouraged and governments assumed the responsibility to provide material relief to the poor.

- With expansion of federal involvement, methods of caring for the poor changed substantially.

- Compared to practices and methods employed in the first hundred years of American history, modern methods have largely discarded the quest to build personal relationships with the poor in order to individualize relief and care, the development and protection of the individual's work ethic, and the enhancement of the individual's moral character that includes the quest to remain financially independent of others.

Chapter 9

The Gap

This book represents a response to the near-incessant disparagement of the rich. It comes in a variety of forms—some direct and some indirect. Often those in the top income distributions are accused of dishonesty, corruption, and unfair dealings. The implication is that they do not deserve the material wealth that has been accrued. Indirect disparagements are more common and focus upon the gap between the rich and the poor. An increasing inequality of income is often viewed as direct evidence of either failures of our free-market-based economy to function properly or a reflection of successful conquests in taking from the poor to enhance the financial status of the rich. Though perhaps centered in secular media and investigative reporting, these discourses find their way into our churches, where they have unintended consequences.

Many from the top income distributions sit with us in our pews on Sundays. Most fade into the congregation without any distinctive appearance or conduct. In most churches, how much anyone gives to the church remains confidential. This, in part, is because these people do not want to be recognized as rich. Yet, the direct disparagements of the rich in the church are experienced by these church members. They are deemed guilty by association without even the thought that higher incomes might have been earned honestly and with integrity.

The secular press is always quick to report on a growing gap between the rich and the poor. These reports, too, find their way into our churches. There is a presumption behind these disparagements of any widening of the gap between the rich and the poor that somehow the poor are injured or disadvantaged as a consequence. Our economists in the prior chapters taught us that a widening gap between the rich and

103

the poor is a positive reflection of economic growth and that economic growth is the single, most effective tool by which poverty is eliminated. The economists note that these conversations are often infected with the ancient notion of a wages fund—a notion rejected centuries ago. In fact, there is not a fixed pool of money to be shared by the rich and the poor. It is not the case that as the rich get more, the poor get less. Instead, changes in the distribution of income occur because of changes in productivity among the sectors of the economy. The pool of money is growing in size. In a developed economy, it would be a rare exception to find that any group became poor because a sector of the economy either became more productive or its products increased in value. Perhaps exceptions can be found, but as a general proposition, economic growth benefits all of society.

Where is the foundation in religious settings from which disparagement of the rich is appropriate and justified? The most often quoted scripture, the rich man seeking salvation, is not a parable that contends that the accumulation of wealth is sinful. Instead, it is a parable reminding us that we do not attain salvation through any merit or work of our own. It is a challenging, if not impossible, task to find in scripture the condemning of higher income attained through honest and diligent work. This thought is not central within scripture.

Our Christian roots began with Jewish doctrine, which is most fully presented in the Mishnah and Talmud, which developed apart from early Christian literature. Jewish doctrine rejects wholesale disparagement of the rich. These roots include the Catholic doctrine, which includes rejections of public policies seeking to narrow the gap between the rich and the poor. Methodist roots include the sermons and hymns of John and Charles Wesley. Wesleyan teachings remind us that there is a natural disparity in ability and motivation, which results in unequal distributions of income. As Christians, we are to earn all we can in order to care for ourselves, members of our households, and, of course, those in poverty. The central message from our religious roots is that we are to work hard and smart in continuing the work of God's creation so that we can better care for the poor and avoid our own financial dependence upon others.

Our nation's history began with charitable efforts that focused upon the material and spiritual needs of the individual. There was great care taken to strengthen the work ethic of the individual—the primary characteristic that enables people to remain financially independent. There was a rejection of indiscriminate distribution of material goods for fear of encouraging a lifestyle of dependency and a loss of the will to improve one's own station in life. In time, these principles have largely been discarded.

Some economists have asserted that churches curtailed works of charity for the poor as governments expanded the welfare state. It is difficult to address the need for spiritual growth among the poor when material needs are met through a host of entitlement programs. Before this happened, churches bundled spiritual care with material support so that both needs could be addressed within broader programs. Today, these opportunities are more difficult to find, and positive outcomes are more difficult to achieve.

I remember the stories of our grandparents who lived on farms and regularly had enough food for the family. Being near the railroad, travelers would make camps nearby and often would approach the farmhouse seeking work for a meal. Regardless of the amount of food on hand, they were never refused. These were pure gestures of kindness with receptions of genuine thankfulness. During the Great Depression there was little loss of the work ethic. There simply were not enough jobs.

With the Great Recession, there was an unprecedented expansion of public assistance, largely uncoupled with any work requirements. How could churches extend relief to those truly in need and encourage work and financial independence? At least two books, *Toxic Charity* and *When Helping Hurts*, underscore the importance of encouraging financial independence.[1]

I am currently on a board of a foundation that distributes grants to churches engaged in care of the least of these. The grants committee chose to terminate the series of grants to a church that was celebrating its food service to the third generation of the same family. Instead, it began a new grant to a church seeking to help families get off public assistance and become productive. Perhaps times are changing.

---

1. Robert D. Lupton, *Toxic Charity: How Churches and Charities Hurt Those They Help, and How to Reverse It* (New York: HarperCollins, 2011); Steve Corbett and Brian Fikkert, *When Helping Hurts: How to Alleviate Poverty Without Hurting the Poor... and Yourself* (Chicago: Moody Publishers, 2012).

In other ways, we have made it more difficult for our churches. We too often disparage the rich as if the attainment of wealth is evidence of dishonesty, corruption, and unfair treatment of others. We too often seek a more equal distribution of income through public policies when such is not achievable and results in slower economic growth, which is harmful to the poor. We too often support expansions of entitlement programs that inhibit effective work of missions through which those in poverty benefit from spiritual development and a stronger sense of personal responsibility. We too often, through our speech, writings, and conduct, offend the rich and make our houses of worship unwelcome places.

Mother Teresa is known to have said that among all people, the rich are most in need of the ministries of the church—not because they are inherently sinful people—but because they face unusually difficult challenges.[2] Perhaps we should gain a deeper understanding of our own religious roots.

---

2.   Lynn Twist, *The Soul of Money* (New York: W. W. Norton, 2003), 35–36.

References

Alvaredo, Facundo, Anthony B. Atkinson, Thomas Piketty, and Emmanuel Saez. "The Top 1 Percent in International and Historical Perspective." *Journal of Economic Perspectives* 27, no. 3 (Summer 2013): 3–20.

Aquinas, St. Thomas. *Summa Theologica*. New York, NY: Benzigor Bros., 1947, 1265–1274.

Barro, Robert J. "Inequality and Growth in a Panel of Countries." *Journal of Economic Growth* 5, no. 1 (2000): 5–32.

Batey, Richard A. *Jesus and the Forgotten City: New Light on Sepphoris and the Urban World of Jesus*. Grand Rapids, MI: Baker Book House, 1991.

Becker, Gary S. "Human Capital." *The Concise Encyclopedia of Economics*. www.econlib.org/library/Enc/HumanCapital.html. Accessed September 5, 2015.

Becker, Gary S. "A Theory of Social Interactions." *Journal of Political Economy* 82, no. 6 (1974): 1063–93.

Becker, Gary S., and Kevin M. Murphy. "The Upside of Income Inequality." *The American* 1, no. 4 (May/June 2007): 20–23.

Block, Walter. *Morality of the Market: Religious and Economic Perspectives*. Vancouver, BC, Canada: Frazer Institute, 1985.

The Book of Discipline of The United Methodist Church. Nashville: The United Methodist Publishing House, 2012.

The Book of Resolutions of The United Methodist Church. Nashville: The United Methodist Publishing House, 2012.

Borg, M. J. *Evolution of the Word: New Testament in the Order the Books Were Written*. New York, NY: Harper Collins, 2012.

Collins, Kenneth J., and Jason E. Vickers, eds. *The Sermons of John*

Wesley: A Collection for the Christian Journey. Nashville: Abingdon Press, 2013.

Corbett, Steve, and Brian Fikkert. *When Helping Hurts: How to Alleviate Poverty without Hurting the Poor . . . and Yourself.* Chicago: Moody Publishers, 2009.

Dollar, David, and Aart Kraay. "Growth Is Good for the Poor." Policy Research Working Paper, no. 2587, Washington, DC: The World Bank, April 2001.

Finke, Roger, and Rodney Stark. *The Churching of America, 1776–2005.* New Brunswick, NJ: Rutgers University Press, 2005.

Friedman, Milton. *Capitalism and Freedom.* Chicago: The University of Chicago Press, 1962.

Galbraith, John Kenneth. *The New Industrial State.* Princeton, NJ: Princeton University Press, 1967.

Gave, Charles. *Jesus, the Unknown Economist.* Central, Hong Kong: GaveKal Research, 2007.

Harrelson, Walter J. *The Ten Commandments and Human Rights.* Macon, GA: Mercer University Press, 1997.

Hayek, F. A. *The Constitution of Liberty.* Chicago: The University of Chicago Press, 1960.

———. *The Fatal Conceit, The Errors of Socialism.* Chicago: The University of Chicago Press, 1989.

———. *Individualism and Economic Order.* Chicago: The University of Chicago, 1948.

———. *The Road to Serfdom.* Chicago: The University of Chicago, 1944.

Jones, Scott J. *United Methodist Doctrine: The Extreme Center.* Nashville: Abingdon Press, 2002.

Kreeft, Peter J. *Catholic Christianity.* Chicago: Ignatius Press, 2001.

Lifshitz, Joseph Isaac. *Judaism, Law & the Free Market: An Analysis.* Grand Rapids: Acton Institute, 2012.

Lupton, Robert D. *Toxic Charity: How Churches and Charities Hurt Those They Help (and How to Reverse It).* New York: Harper One, 2011.

Maccoby, Hyam. *Judaism on Trial: Jewish-Christian Disputations in the Middle Ages.* Oxford, England: The Littman Library of Jewish Civilization, 1982.

Marshall, Alfred. *Principles of Economics*, 8th ed. London: Macmillan & Co., 1964.

Mill, John Steward. *Principles of Political Economy.* Edited by W. J. Ashley. New York, NY: Augustus M. Kelley, Publishers, 1965.

New Revised Standard Version Wesley Study Bible. Nashville: Abingdon Press, 2009.

Novak, Michael. *The Catholic Ethic and the Spirit of Capitalism.* New York: Free Press, 1993.

Olasky, Marvin. *The Tragedy of American Compassion.* Wheaton, IL: Crossway Books, 1992.

Outler, Albert, ed. *John Wesley.* New York: Oxford University Press, 1964.

Ramsey, Dave. *The Legacy Journey.* Brentwood, TN: Ramsey Press, 2014.

Ravallion, Martin. "Inequality Is Bad for the Poor," World Bank Policy Research Working Paper, no. 3677, Washington, DC: The World Bank, August 2005.

Sauer, Corinne, and Robert M. Sauer. *Judaism, Markets, and Capitalism: Separating Myth from Reality.* Grand Rapids: Acton Institute, 2006.

Saving, Thomas R. *Live Free and Prosper.* Private Enterprise Research Center, Texas A&M University, College Station, TX, 2015.

Sirico, Father Robert. *Defending the Free Market: The Moral Case for a Free Economy.* Grand Rapids: Acton Institute, 2013.

Stiglitz, Joseph E. *The Price of Inequality: How Today's Divided Society Endangers Our Future.* New York: W. W. Norton and Company, 2012.

Tamari, Meir. *With All Your Possessions: Jewish Ethics and Economic Life.* Jerusalem: Maggid Books, 2014.

Telushkin, Rabbi Joseph. *Jewish Literacy: The Most Important Things to Know about the Jewish Religion, Its People, and Its History.* New York: William Morrow and Company, 1991.

Twist, Lynne. *The Soul of Money: Reclaiming the Wealth of Our Inner Resources.* New York: W. W. Norton and Company, 2003.

Webber, Max. *The Protestant Ethic and the Spirit of Capitalism and Other Writings.* New York, NY: Penguin Books, 2002.

Woods, Thomas E., Jr. *The Church and the Market: A Catholic Defense of the Free Economy.* New York: Lexington Books, 2005.